FRENCH
IN 3 MONTHS

Ronald Overy and Jacqueline Lecanuet

YOUR ESSENTIAL GUIDE TO UNDERSTANDING AND SPEAKING FRENCH

FREE AUDIO APP

THIRD EDITION
Series Editor Elise Bradbury
Senior Editor Amelia Petersen
Senior Art Editor Jane Ewart
Managing Editors Christine Stroyan, Carine Tracanelli
Managing Art Editor Anna Hall
Production Editor Jacqueline Street-Elkayam
Senior Production Controller Samantha Cross
Jacket Project Art Editor Surabhi Wadhwa-Gandhi
Jacket Design Development Manager Sophia MTT
Art Director Karen Self
Associate Publishing Director Liz Wheeler
Publishing Director Jonathan Metcalf

DK INDIA
Project Art Editor Anjali Sachar
Senior DTP Designer Shanker Prasad
Managing Editor Rohan Sinha
Managing Art Editor Sudakshina Basu

This American Edition, 2022
First American Edition, 1997
Published in the United States by DK Publishing,
a division of Penguin Random House LLC
1745 Broadway, 20th Floor, New York, NY 10019

Copyright © 1997, 2003, 2022 Dorling Kindersley Limited
24 25 10 9 8 7 6
006–326774–Jan/2022

Written by
Ronald Overy F.I.L.
Formerly Senior Lecturer at The Language Centre, South Bank Polytechnic, London
and
Jacqueline Lecanuet L. ès L., PG Dip. Ling.
Formerly Principal Lecturer in French at The School of International Business and Languages,
South Bank University, London

A catalog record for this book is available from the Library of Congress.
ISBN 978-0-7440-5160-5

DK books are available at special discounts when purchased in bulk for sales promotions,
premiums, fund-raising, or educational use. For details, contact:
DK Publishing Special Markets,
1745 Broadway, 20th Floor, New York, NY 10019
SpecialSales@dk.com

Printed and bound in China

www.dk.com

MIX
Paper | Supporting
responsible forestry
FSC™ C018179

This book was made with Forest
Stewardship Council™ certified
paper – one small step in DK's
commitment to a sustainable future.
Learn more at
www.dk.com/uk/information/sustainability

Preface

Hugo French in 3 Months has been written by two lecturers whose combined experience in teaching French ranges from beginners to postgraduate level. Both authors taught at the South Bank Polytechnic, now London South Bank University, where Jacqueline Lecanuet was Principal Lecturer in French. Her husband, Ronald Overy, was an inspired teacher and author of textbooks in French, Spanish, and Russian.

The course begins with an explanation of French pronunciation, as far as this is possible in print. We strongly encourage you to download the free *DK Hugo in 3 Months* app (see p.4) and you can listen to the accompanying audio as you work through the course—this will enable you to pick up the distinctive sounds of the French language. Referring to our system of "imitated pronunciation" will also help you learn to pronounce French accurately and understand it when you hear it.

It has always been a principle of the Hugo method to teach only what is really essential. We assume that the student wants to learn French from a practical standpoint, so the lessons contain the most useful grammatical rules. Constructions are clearly explained, and the order in which the explanations are given allows rapid progress for learners who study regularly.

Each week includes exercises to practice what you've learned along with the vocabulary you need to complete them. Conversations offer examples of everyday French, as it is spoken. The course finishes with a piece of text for reading practice, along with the English translation.

Ideally, you should spend about an hour a day on your work, although there is no hard-and-fast rule on this. Do as much as you feel capable of doing; it is much better to learn a little at a time and to learn that thoroughly.

Before beginning a new section, always spend 10 minutes studying what you learned the day before. Then read each new section carefully, ensuring that you have fully understood the grammar, before listening to the audio to learn the pronunciation of sample sentences and new vocabulary. Finally, complete the exercises that accompany each section. Repeat them until the answers come easily. With the conversations, we suggest that you listen to them first, then read them aloud and see how closely you can imitate the voices on the recording. Repetition is vital to language learning. The more often you listen to a conversation or repeat an oral exercise, the more your skills will improve.

When you've completed the course, you should have a very good understanding of the language—more than sufficient for general vacation or business purposes, and enough to support you in language validation tests if that is your aim. It is important to continue expanding your vocabulary by reading in French or watching French films—or, best of all, visiting France or Canada.

We hope you enjoy *Hugo French in 3 Months*, and we wish you success with your studies!

About the audio app

The audio app that accompanies this French course contains audio recordings for all numbered sections, vocabulary boxes, conversations, and most of the exercises. There is no audio for the Self-assessment tests or Reading Practice section.

◀✕ Where you see this symbol, it indicates that there is no audio for that section.

To start using the audio with this book, go to **www.dk.com/hugo** and download the *DK Hugo in 3 Months* app on your smartphone or tablet from the App Store or Google Play. Then, select French from the list of titles.

Please note that this app is not a standalone course. It is designed to be used together with the book, to familiarize you with French speech and to provide examples for you to repeat aloud.

Contents

Pronunciation

French is a very pleasant-sounding language, but it can present English speakers with one or two problems from the point of view of pronunciation.

Hugo's method of imitated pronunciation is sufficiently accurate for you to make yourself understood. Naturally, however, the best way to acquire good pronunciation is to practice with the audio that accompanies the course. This will allow you to hear the words and phrases as you follow them in the book.

Although French spelling may appear complicated, it still remains a better guide to how words are actually spoken than English spelling occasionally is!

Read through the following rules and advice on French pronunciation, but there is no need to learn these by heart; just refer back to them whenever you need to, and you'll soon become familiar with them.

WORD STRESS

Unlike English, all syllables in French words are distinctly sounded and evenly stressed, with a little more emphasis being given to the last syllable. Contrast the stress in the word "important," which appears below in both languages:

English: im-POR-tant French: a*ng*-por-tah*ng*

PRONUNCIATION OF VOWELS

a	is pronounced like "ah" in English	**la** (the)
à	is also pronounced like "ah"	**là** (there)
â	is also pronounced like "ah"	**âne** (donkey)
e	in the middle of a syllable is pronounced like "ai" in "fair"	**mer** (sea)
e	at the end of a syllable is pronounced like "uh" in "the"	**le** (the)

e	is silent at the end of a word	**tasse** (cup)
é	is pronounced like "ay"	**été** (summer)
è	is pronounced like "ai" in "fair"	**père** (father)
ê	is pronounced like "e" in "let"	**tête** (head)
i, y	are pronounced like "ee" in "meet"	**ski** (skiing), **y** (there)
o	is pronounced like "o" in "cold"	**poste** (post office)
ô	is pronounced like "oh"	**hôtel**
u	this sound does not exist in English; say "ee" with pursed lips	**vu** (seen)
oi	is pronounced like "wah"	**roi** (king)
ou	is pronounced like "oo"	**roue** (wheel)
ai, ei	are pronounced like "e" in "let"	**laine** (wool), **reine** (queen)
au, eau	are pronounced like "oh"	**au** (to the), **eau** (water)
eu, œu	are pronounced like "uh" in "the"	**neuf** (nine), **sœur** (sister)

PRONUNCIATION OF CONSONANTS

French consonants are generally pronounced as in English, but note the following:

c	before e or i sounds like "s"	**ceci** (this)
c	elsewhere sounds like "k"	**car** (coach)

ç	sounds like "s"	**ça** (that)
ch	sounds like "sh"	**château** (castle)
g	before e or i sounds like "zh" in "measure"	**général** (general)
g	elsewhere sounds like "g" in "go"	**gare** (station)
h	is silent	**hôtel**
j	sounds like "zh" in "measure"	**je** (I)
qu, q	sound like "k"	**qui** (who)
r	is pronounced at the back of the throat; something like the sound made when gargling	**rire** (to laugh)
s	at the beginning of a word sounds like "s"	**salle** (room)
s	between two vowels sounds like "z"	**rose** (rose)

IMPORTANT: With the exception of c, f, l, and r, consonants are not usually pronounced when they are the last letter in a word: **passepor(t)**, **Pari(s)** BUT **hôtel**, **professeur**.

NASAL SOUNDS

These sounds are very characteristic of the French language, but we have nasal sounds in English, too: compare "sing," "sang," "sung," "song"—remembering that the standard pronunciation gives very little value to the g. French has four very similar nasal sounds, which we show as *ng* in the "imitated pronunciation" (see page 12):

om, on	pronounce like o*ng* in "song"	**nom** (name), **non** (no)

um*, un	pronounce like u*ng* in "sung"	**un** (one), **brun** (brown)
am, an, em, en	pronounce like "ah*ng*"	**champ** (field), **an** (year) **temps** (time), **en** (in)
im*, in, aim, ain, ein	pronounce like a*ng* in "sang"	**simple** (easy), **vin** (wine), **faim** (hunger), **bain** (bath), **plein** (full)
ien	pronounce like "ee-a*ng*"	**bien** (well)

*Some French speakers make no distinction between these two sounds and pronounce them both like a*ng* in "sang."

VARIATIONS

er	at the end of a word of two syllables or more sounds like "ay"	**parler** (to speak)
ez	at the end of a word sounds like "ay"	**nez** (nose)
ail	at the end of a word sounds like "ah-ee"	**travail** (work)
eil, eille	sound like "a-ee"	**soleil** (sun), **bouteille** (bottle)
ill	usually sounds like "ee-y"	**billet** (ticket)
gn	sounds like "nyuh" in "onion"	**signal** (signal)

LIAISON

The French like their language to flow smoothly. For this reason, if a word beginning with a vowel or a silent h follows a word ending in a consonant, this consonant is linked to the beginning of the second word:

nous‿avons (noo zah-vo*ng*), we have
un petit‿enfant (u*ng* p'tee tah*ng*-fah*ng*), a small child

When carried over in this way:

s, x sound like "z": **deux‿ans** (duh zah*ng*), two years

d sounds like "t": **un grand‿arbre** (u*ng* grah*ng* tahbruh), a tall tree

f sounds like "v": **neuf‿heures** (nuh vuhr), nine hours

ACCENTS

There are three main accents in French: the acute (**é**), found on the letter e; the grave (**è**), found on a, e, and u; and the circumflex (**ê**), found on any vowel. There is also the cedilla (**ç**), found only underneath the letter c.

The function of the accents is:

1. To modify the sound of a letter. The unaccented **e** sounds like "uh" in "the," the **é** acute sounds like "ay" in "say," and the **è** grave sounds like "ai" in "fair."

The **c** that would be hard before an a or o (as in "car") is softened to sound like "s" in "sit" when it has a cedilla (**garçon**, "boy").

2. To distinguish between words with the same spelling but a different meaning. For example, **la** (the), **là** (there); **ou** (or), **où** (where); **sur** (on), **sûr** (sure).

Sometimes French accents are not printed when they appear above a capital letter.

THE IMITATED PRONUNCIATION

Pronounce all syllables as if they formed part of an English word, giving equal stress to each syllable, but note the following:

ng (italics)	must never be pronounced; these letters merely indicate that the preceding vowel has a nasal sound
uh	is an unstressed vowel sound something like "e" in "the" or "a" in "about"
zh	sounds like "s" in "measure"
ü	no equivalent in English; purse your lips and say "ee"
o	a closed "o" something like "cold"
oh	an open "o" like "go" or "note"

THE FRENCH ALPHABET

This is the same as in English, but K and W are not used much. You should know how to pronounce the letters in case you have to spell out a word such as your name: H-A-L-E-Y would be spelled as "ahsh ah el uh ee-grek," for example.

A	(ah)	**H**	(ahsh)	**O**	(oh)	**V**	(vay)
B	(bay)	**I**	(ee)	**P**	(pay)	**W**	(doobluh-vay)
C	(say)	**J**	(zhee)	**Q**	(kü)	**X**	(eeks)
D	(day)	**K**	(kah)	**R**	(airr)	**Y**	(ee-grek)
E	(uh)	**L**	(el)	**S**	(ess)	**Z**	(zed)
F	(ef)	**M**	(em)	**T**	(tay)		
G	(zhay)	**N**	(en)	**U**	(ü)		

PUNCTUATION

In standard written French, a space is left before punctuation marks that have more than one element (e.g. ?). This book follows English punctuation rules.

Week 1

- How to say "the," "a," and "some"
- How to recognize whether a noun is masculine or feminine, and which article to use with each gender
- Formation of the plural
- How to say "I," "you," "he," "she," "it," "we," "they"
- Simple greetings and forms of address
- The present tense of **avoir**, "to have"
- Formation of the negative

1.1 ARTICLES: THE, A, AN, SOME

In French, all nouns have a gender—they are either masculine or feminine. Articles change depending on the gender of the noun that follows and whether it is singular or plural.

"The" is expressed by:

le (masculine singular)	**le passeport** the passport
la (feminine singular)	**la leçon** the lesson
l' (before a vowel or h*)	**l'imprimante** the printer
	l'hôtel the hotel
les (m. and f. plural)	**les passeports** the passports

*Note that a few words beginning with h take **le**, **la**.

"A" or "an" are expressed by:

un (masculine singular)	**un livre** a book
une (feminine singular)	**une lettre** a letter

"Some" or "any" are expressed by:

du (masculine singular)	**du vin** some wine
de la (feminine singular)	**de la bière** some beer
de l' (before a vowel or h)	**de l'alcool** some alcohol
des (m. and f. plural)	**des leçons** some lessons

Note: **du** and **des** are both contractions:
de + le = du; de + les = des

1

Sometimes "some" and "any" are omitted in English, but they must always be expressed in French:

we have wine = **nous avons <u>du</u> vin**

IMITATED PRONUNCIATION

luh pahs-porr; lah luh-song; lang-pree-mahnt; loh-tel; lay pahs-porr; u*ng* leevruh; ün letruh; dü va*ng*; duh lah bee-airr; duh lahl-kol; day luh-so*ng*; noo zah-vo*ng* dü va*ng*

1.2 GENDER OF NOUNS

Unfortunately, there are few rules that can help determine the gender of French nouns. The best solution is to always try to learn each noun and its gender together. Generally speaking, **-e** and **-ion** are feminine endings, although there are exceptions. Nouns denoting males are generally masculine, and those referring to females are usually feminine:

le monsieur gentleman
le journal newspaper
le parfum perfume
le château castle
le neveu nephew
le prix price
l'autobus (m.) bus

la dame lady
la valise suitcase
la station station

le journaliste male journalist
la journaliste female journalist

Occasionally, only one gender exists and this has to be used irrespective of the sex of the person: for example, **la personne** (person) is always feminine. However, today even invariable nouns that don't change according to the gender of the person referred to are distinguished by the article: for example, **le/la témoin** (witness).

IMITATED PRONUNCIATION

muhs-yuh; zhoor-nahl; pahr-fu*ng*; shah-toh; nuh-vuh; pree; oh-toh-büs; dahm; vah-leez; stahs-yo*ng*; zhoor-nah-leest; pairr-sonn; tay-mwah*ng*

1.3 PLURAL OF NOUNS

The plural is formed:

1. By adding **s**:

valise (suitcase) becomes **valises**

2. By adding **x** to words ending in **au** or **eu**:

château (castle) becomes **châteaux**
neveu (nephew) becomes **neveux**

3. By changing the ending **al** to **aux**:

journal (newspaper) becomes **journaux**

Words ending in **s** and **x** do not change:

autobus (bus or buses); **prix** (price or prices)

IMITATED PRONUNCIATION

vah-leez; shah-toh; nuh-vuh; zhoor-nahl; zhoor-noh; oh-toh-büs; pree

Exercise 1

◀×

Translate the following:

1. the passport
2. the hotel
3. the suitcase
4. a station
5. a lesson
6. a book
7. a person
8. the journalists
9. the prices
10. some beer
11. some wine
12. some letters
13. some newspapers
14. some buses

1.4 SUBJECT PRONOUNS: I, YOU, SHE, HE, ETC.

singular		plural	
je	I	**nous**	we
tu	you (familiar)	**vous**	you (familiar)
vous	you (formal)	**vous**	you (formal)
il	he, it (m.)	**ils**	they (m.)
elle	she, it (f.)	**elles**	they (f.)

Note: **je** becomes **j'** before a vowel or h.

1.5 ADDRESSING PEOPLE

English, on occasion, can be a very straightforward language. Whether we are talking to a dog, a friend, our husband or wife, or our boss, we use the same word: "you." In French, it's not quite so simple because there are two words for "you"—**tu** and **vous**—and their use depends on who you are addressing.

1

The French use **tu** when talking to a friend, a relative, a child, or someone they are on friendly terms with. Note that **tu** is used only to address one person—to address more than one person, **vous** is used in any circumstance, familiar or formal. Today, young people often use **tu** with each other even on the first meeting, and informal workplaces adopt **tu** between colleagues.

In cases in which you don't know someone well, it's best to start by using the more formal **vous**. In the exercises in this book, unless indicated otherwise (by "familiar" in brackets), use **vous** for "you."

All of the above regarding **tu** and **vous** also applies to words such as **te** (you), **ton** (your), **votre** (your), etc.

The words **Monsieur**, **Madame**, and **Mademoiselle** mean Mr., Mrs., and Miss and are placed, as in English, before a surname:

Monsieur Dupont, Madame Duval, Mademoiselle Martin

The French also use these titles a great deal in formal conversation without a name:

Bonjour, monsieur.	Good morning, good afternoon (to a man)
Bonsoir, madame.	Good evening (to a woman)
Au revoir, mademoiselle.	Goodbye (to a young woman)

Monsieur, madame, and **mademoiselle** also have a plural form: **messieurs, mesdames, mesdemoiselles**.

There is no French equivalent of "Ms.," but these days **Madame** is increasingly used to address all women, married or otherwise, to avoid any hint of sexism.

IMITATED PRONUNCIATION

zhuh; tü; voo; eel; el; noo; voo; voo; eel; el; muh-yuh
dü-po*ng*; mah-dahm dü-vahl; mahd-mwah-zel
mahr-ta*ng*; bo*ng*-zhoor, muhs-yuh; bo*ng*-swahr,
mah-dahm; orr-vwahrr, mahd-mwah-zel; mays-yuh;
may-dahm; mayd-mwah-zel

1.6 AVOIR ("TO HAVE")

This is one of the most important French verbs, so it
should be learned early on.

Present tense

j'ai	I have
tu as	you have (familiar sing.)
il a, elle a	he/it (m.) has, she/it (f.) has
nous avons	we have
vous avez	you have (formal sing. and all pl.)
ils ont, elles ont	they (m.) have, they (f.) have

VOCABULARY 1

Study these words:

le livre	book
l'appareil-photo (m.)	camera
la tablette	tablet
la carte	map, card
la clé	key
la voiture	car
la radio	radio
oui	yes
non	no
et	and

IMITATED PRONUNCIATION

ah-vwahr; zhay; tü ah; eel ah; el ah; noo zah-vo*ng*; voo
zah-vay; eel zo*ng*; el zo*ng*; leevruh; ah-pah-ray'ee fo-toh;
tah-blett; kahrt; klay; vwah-tür; rad-yoh; wee; no*ng*; ay

Exercise 2

Answer the questions as follows:

Pierre a du vin? Does Pierre have any wine?
Oui, il a du vin. Yes, he has some wine.

1. Nicole a un journal?
2. Sophie et Pierre ont une voiture?
3. Vous avez une radio?
4. Vous avez une carte?
5. Nous avons une clé?
6. J'ai une tablette?

THE NEGATIVE

"Not" is expressed by **ne** placed before the verb and **pas**
after; **ne** becomes **n'** before a vowel or h:

je n'ai pas	I have not
tu n'as pas	you have not (familiar sing.)
il n'a pas	he/it (m.) has not
elle n'a pas	she/it (f.) has not
nous n'avons pas	we have not
vous n'avez pas	you have not (form. sing. and pl.)
ils n'ont pas	they (m.) have not
elles n'ont pas	they (f.) have not

After a negative, **un, une, du, de la, de l'**, and **des**
change to **de** (**d'** before a vowel or h).

J'ai de la bière.	I have some beer.
Je n'ai pas de bière.	I have no beer.

IMITATED PRONUNCIATION

zhuh nay pah; tü nah pah; eel nah pah; el nah pah;
noo nah-vong pah; voo nah-vay pah; eel nong pah;
el nong pah; zhay duh lah bee-airr; zhuh nay pah duh
bee-airr

WEEK 1   19

Exercise 3

Answer the questions as follows:

Vous avez une voiture?   Do you have a car?
Non, je n'ai pas de voiture.   No, I don't have a car.

1. Vous avez une valise?
2. Vous avez un passeport?
3. Nous avons du vin?
4. Nous avons un livre?
5. Paul a des tablettes?
6. Anne-Marie a une radio?
7. J'ai des journaux?
8. Elles ont un appareil-photo?

Exercise 4

Translate:

1. I have a car.
2. I do not have any keys.
3. We have a suitcase.
4. She has some alcohol.
5. He does not have a newspaper.
6. They (m.) have some books.
7. They (f.) do not have any maps.
8. You do not have a printer.
9. Do you have a camera?
10. Do you have any tablets?
11. Do you have any books?
12. Do you have a radio?

VOCABULARY 2

à	at, to
au (à + le = au)	at the
le contrôle	control, check
le policier/ la policière	police officer (m./f.)
l'instant (m.)	moment
le miracle	miracle
le/la touriste	tourist (m./f.)
le portable	mobile phone
la clé USB	USB flash drive
attendez	wait (formal and pl.)
c'est	this is, that is
s'il vous plaît	please (formal)
voici	here is, here are
où	where
très	very
grave	serious
peut-être	perhaps
mais	but
Mince!	Oh no!, Oh dear!
aussi	also

IMITATED PRONUNCIATION

ah; oh; kong-trohl; po-lees-yay/yairr; ang-stahng;
mee-rahkluh; too-reest; porr-tahbluh; klay oo-ess-bay;
say; seel voo play; vwah-see; oo; tray; grahv; puh-
tetruh; may; mangs; oh-see

CONVERSATION

Au contrôle des passeports

POLICIER   **Votre passeport, s'il vous plaît, madame.**

TOURISTE   **Un instant, s'il vous plaît.**
[She searches in her handbag.]
Mon passeport? Où est mon passeport?
Et mince alors! J'ai un livre, une carte de
France, des clés, un portable, mais ... je n'ai
pas de passeport!

POLICIER   **Vous n'avez pas de passeport, madame?**
C'est très grave. Mais votre passeport est
peut-être dans la valise?

TOURISTE   **Attendez, monsieur.**
[She searches in her suitcase.]
J'ai un appareil-photo, une clé USB, et une
tablette. J'ai aussi du vin, du parfum, un
journal ....

POLICIER   **Vous permettez, madame?**
[He searches in her suitcase.]
Voici l'appareil-photo, le journal, le vin, le
parfum, et la tablette. Et ... miracle—voici
le passeport!

At passport control

OFFICER   Your passport please, madam.

TOURIST   One moment, please.
[She searches in her handbag.]
My passport? Where's my passport? Oh no! I've got a book, a map of France, some keys, a mobile phone, but ... I don't have a passport!

OFFICER   You don't have your passport, madam? That's very serious. But perhaps your passport is in the suitcase?

TOURIST   Wait.
[She searches in her suitcase.]
I have camera, a flash drive, and a tablet. I also have some wine, some perfume, a newspaper ....

OFFICER   May I?
[He searches in her suitcase.]
Here's the camera, the newspaper, the wine, the perfume, and the tablet. And ... surprise—here's the passport!

Week 2

- How to say "I am," "you are," etc.—the present tense of **être**
- Some common adjectives, and how they agree in number and gender with the noun they describe
- The present tense of regular verbs ending in **-er**
- A variety of ways to frame a question
- Numbers 0–15

2.1 ÊTRE ("TO BE")

This is another very important verb and should be learned early on, as you'll use it a lot!

je suis	I am
tu es	you are (familiar sing.)
il est	he/it (m.) is
elle est	she/it (f.) is
nous sommes	we are
vous êtes	you are (formal sing. and all pl.)
ils sont	they are (m.)
elles sont	they are (f.)

IMITATED PRONUNCIATION
zhuh swee; tü ay; eel ay; el ay; noo som; voo zet; eel song; el song

VOCABULARY 1

Study these professions (m./f.):

le/la médecin	doctor
le banquier/la banquière	banker
le/la pilote	pilot
le professeur/ la professeur(e)	teacher
l'avocat/l'avocate	lawyer
le/la journaliste	journalist
le/la secrétaire	secretary
l'astronaute (m./f.)	astronaut

NOTE: When talking about their profession, the French omit the "a/an" and say "I am doctor," "I am pilot," etc.:

je suis médecin, je suis pilote

IMITATED PRONUNCIATION

med-sa*ng*; bah*ng*k-yay/yairr; pee-lot; pro-fess-uhr; ah-vo-kah/kaht; zhoor-nah-leest; suh-kray-tairr; ah-stro-noht

Exercise 1

Translate:

1. I am a doctor.
2. He is a pilot.
3. She is a journalist.
4. We are bankers.
5. You (m.) are a lawyer.
6. They (f.) are teachers.
7. They (m.) are astronauts.

2.2 ADJECTIVES

French adjectives have both a masculine and a feminine form, singular and plural. The feminine is normally formed by adding **e**. (Adjectives already ending in e do not change.) In the plural, an **s** is usually added:

Il est intelligent. He is intelligent.
Elle est intelligente. She is intelligent.
Je suis grand. I (m.) am tall.
Je suis grande. I (f.) am tall.
Ils sont petits. They (m.) are small.
Elles sont petites. They (f.) are small.

NOTE: The addition of the **e** results in the preceding consonant being pronounced.

Adjectives ending in **x** change the **x** to **se** in the feminine:

dangereux (dangerous) becomes **dangereuse**.

Additional rules for forming the feminine of adjectives:

Final **f** changes to **ve**: **attentif, attentive** (f.)—attentive

Final **er** changes to **ère**: **premier, première** (f.)—first

Final **et** changes to **ète**: **secret, secrète** (f.)—secret

VOCABULARY 2

riche	rich	**stupide**	stupid
pauvre	poor	**poli**	polite
facile	easy	**impoli**	impolite
difficile	difficult	**heureux**	happy
intéressant	interesting	**malheureux**	unhappy
ennuyeux	boring	**bon, bonne** (f.)	good
intelligent	intelligent	**mauvais**	bad

IMITATED PRONUNCIATION

a*ng*-tel-ee-zhah*ng*; a*ng*-tel-ee-zhah*ng*t; grah*ng*; grah*ng*d; p'tee; p'teet; dah*ng*-zhuh-ruh; dah*ng*-zhuh-ruhz; ah-tah*ng*-teef; ah-tah*ng*-teev; pruhm-yay; pruhm-yairr; suhkray; suhkret; reesh; pohv-ruh; fah-seel; dee-fee-seel; a*ng*-tay-ress-ah*ng*; ah*ng*-nwee-yuh; stü-peed; po-lee; *ang*-po-lee; uh-ruh; mahl-uh-ruh; bo*ng*; bonn; moh-vay

Exercise 2

Give the opposite of:

1. Le banquier est riche.
2. La secrétaire est intelligente.
3. Les médecins sont heureux.
4. Les journaux sont intéressants.
5. Le vin est bon.
6. Le livre est facile.
7. L'avocate est polie.
8. La bière est mauvaise.

2

2.3 REGULAR VERBS ENDING IN -ER

The infinitive (the basic form of a verb, e.g. to have, to be) of most French verbs ends in **-er**:

préparer	to prepare
habiter	to live
travailler	to work
parler	to speak
pratiquer	to practice
regarder	to watch
écouter	to listen (to)

The present tense is formed by removing the **-er** from the infinitive and adding the following endings:

je	-e	**nous**	-ons
tu	-es	**vous**	-ez
il/elle	-e	**ils/elles**	-ent

je parle	I speak
tu parles	you speak (fam.)
il parle	he speaks
elle parle	she speaks

nous parlons	we speak
vous parlez	you speak (formal sing. and all pl.)
ils parlent	they speak (m.)
elles parlent	they speak (f.)

The French **je parle**, **il parle**, etc. translates all forms of the English present tense, i.e. I speak, I'm speaking, and sometimes even the near future (more on this later!)

IMITATED PRONUNCIATION

pray-pah-ray; ah-bee-tay; trah-vah'ee-yay; pahr-lay; prah-tee-kay; ruh-gahr-day; ay-koo-tay; zhuh pahrl; tü pahrl; eel pahrl; el pahrl; noo pahr-lo*ng*; voo pahr-lay; eel pahrl; el pahrl

VOCABULARY 3

à	in, at
voyager	to travel
	(**nous voyageons**; see section 12.5 for details about spelling changes)
le sport	sport
la langue	language
la télévision	television
la radio	radio
l'enquête (f.)	survey
deux	two

IMITATED PRONUNCIATION

ah; vwah-yah-zhay; sporr; lah*ng*g; tay-lay-vee-zee-o*ng*; rahd-yoh; ah*ng*-ket; duh

Exercise 3

Complete these sentences:

1. Nous (live) à Versailles.
2. Elle (works) à Nice.
3. Il (travels).
4. Je (speak) deux langues.
5. Elles (practice) un sport.
6. Ils (watch) la télévision.
7. Vous (listen to) la radio.
8. Nous (prepare) une enquête.

2

2.4 ASKING QUESTIONS

In French, you can ask a question:

1. By using a rising intonation—contrast:

Vous parlez français. You speak French. (statement)
Vous parlez français? Do you speak French? (question)

2. By using **est-ce que** (**est-ce qu'** before a vowel or h):

Est-ce que nous travaillons?
Are we working?
Est-ce qu'elle écoute la radio?
Is she listening to the radio?

3. By putting the pronoun after the verb:

Voyagez-vous beaucoup?
Do you travel a great deal?

In this case, if the third-person singular of the verb ends in a vowel, a **t** is inserted between it and the pronoun:
Fume-t-il? Does he smoke?

Note: examples 1 and 2 are less formal than 3 and are used more in spoken language.

VOCABULARY 4

téléphoner	to telephone
réserver	to reserve
exporter	to export
importer	to import
voter	to vote
inviter à dîner	to invite to dinner
il y a	there is, there are
l'hôtel (m.)	hotel
le directeur/la directrice	director
l'ordinateur (m.)	computer
le président/la présidente	president
la chambre	bedroom
la voiture	car
dans	in
de	of
en France	in France, to France

IMITATED PRONUNCIATION

frah*ng*-say; ess-kuh; boh-koo; füm-teel; tay-lay-fo-nay;
ray-zairr-vay; eks-porr-tay; a*ng*-porr-tay; vo-tay;
a*ng*-vee-tay ah dee-nay; eel yah; oh-tel; dee-rek-tuhr/
treece; orr-dee-nah-tuhr; pray-zee-dah*ng*/dah*ng*t;
shah*ng*bruh; vwah-tür; dah*ng*; duh; ah*ng* frah*ng*s

Exercise 4

Using **est-ce que**, ask your friend whether he/she …

1. is telephoning the hotel. (say *to* the hotel)
2. is reserving a room.
3. is inviting the director (m.) to dinner.

Using a rising intonation, ask about Nicole …

4. Is she intelligent?
5. Is she interesting?
6. Is she tall?

Using the inverted form, ask about Peter …

7. Does he export computers to France?
8. Does he import cars?
9. Does he vote for the president?

2.5 NUMBERS

Here are the numbers 0–15:

0	zéro	8	huit
1	un	9	neuf
2	deux	10	dix
3	trois	11	onze
4	quatre	12	douze
5	cinq	13	treize
6	six	14	quatorze
7	sept	15	quinze

IMITATED PRONUNCIATION

zay-roh; u*ng*; duh; trwah; kah-truh; sa*ng*k; sees; set; weet; nuhf; dees; o*ng*z; dooz; trez; kah-torrz; ka*ng*z

Exercise 5

Complete the following, writing the answers in words:

a. 7 + 2 =   e. 10 + 5 =
b. 8 − 6 =   f. 14 − 2 =
c. 3 × 4 =   g. 2 × 7 =
d. 2 + 3 =   h. 2 + 1 =

VOCABULARY 5

sur	on
pour	for
beaucoup	a great deal
seulement	only
souvent	often
jamais	never
plusieurs	several
l'anglais (m.)	English (the language)
le jogging	jogging
l'agence (f.)	agency
la publicité	advertising
la question	question
les affaires (f.)	business
faire	to do, to make

IMITATED PRONUNCIATION

sürr; poorr; boh-koo; suhl-mahng; soo-vahng; zhah-may; plüz-yuhr; ahng-glay; zhog-ing; ah-zhahngs; pü-blee-see-tay; kest-yong; ah-fairr; fairr

CONVERSATION

A French radio reporter is preparing a survey on the French. He's interviewing passersby in the street.

2

JOURNALISTE	**Pardon madame, vous êtes française?**
PASSANTE	**Oui, je suis française.**
JOURNALISTE	**Je prépare une enquête sur les français. J'ai sept questions.**
PASSANTE	**Oui.**
JOURNALISTE	**Vous habitez à Paris?**
PASSANTE	**Non, j'habite à Versailles.**
JOURNALISTE	**Vous travaillez à Paris?**
PASSANTE	**Oui, je travaille pour une agence de publicité.**
JOURNALISTE	**Est-ce que vous voyagez beaucoup?**
PASSANTE	**Oui, je voyage pour affaires.**
JOURNALISTE	**Est-ce que vous parlez plusieurs langues?**
PASSANTE	**Deux seulement, français et anglais.**
JOURNALISTE	**Pratiquez-vous un sport?**
PASSANTE	**Oui, je fais du jogging.**
JOURNALISTE	**Regardez-vous la télévision?**
PASSANTE	**Oui, souvent.**
JOURNALISTE	**Vous écoutez la radio?**
PASSANTE	**Jamais!**

NOTE: Except when referring to the people of a country, adjectives denoting nationality do not take a capital letter: "un hôtel français" (likewise for nouns referring to languages: "je parle anglais"); however, "les français," the French.

2

JOURNALIST	Excuse me, madam, are you French?
PASSERBY	Yes, I'm French.
JOURNALIST	I'm preparing a survey on the French. I have seven questions.
PASSERBY	Yes.
JOURNALIST	Do you live in Paris?
PASSERBY	No, I live in Versailles.
JOURNALIST	Do you work in Paris?
PASSERBY	Yes, I work for an advertising agency.
JOURNALIST	Do you travel a great deal?
PASSERBY	Yes, I travel on business.
JOURNALIST	Do you speak several languages?
PASSERBY	Only two, French and English.
JOURNALIST	Do you practice a sport?
PASSERBY	Yes, I go jogging.
JOURNALIST	Do you watch television?
PASSERBY	Yes, often.
JOURNALIST	Do you listen to the radio?
PASSERBY	Never!

Week 3

- Regular verbs ending in **-ir** and their present tense
- Demonstrative adjectives: "this", "that", "these", "those"
- Some useful expressions using **avoir**
- More about negative forms
- Using question words: "where?", "when?", "how?", etc.
- The imperative in its simplest form

3.1 REGULAR VERBS ENDING IN -IR

The infinitive of a large number of French verbs ends in **-ir**:

finir	to finish
garantir	to guarantee
choisir	to choose
grossir	to put on weight
maigrir	to lose weight
remplir	to fill
réussir	to succeed

The present tense is formed by removing the **-ir** from the infinitive and adding the endings:

je	**-is**	**nous**	**-issons**
tu	**-is**	**vous**	**-issez**
il/elle	**-it**	**ils/elles**	**-issent**

je finis	I finish
tu finis	you finish (familiar)
il finit	he/it finishes
elle finit	she/it finishes
nous finissons	we finish
vous finissez	you finish (formal sing. and all pl.)
ils finissent (m.)	they finish
elles finissent (f.)	they finish

NOTE: Remember that the singular form **tu** is used only with those you're on familiar terms with.

IMITATED PRONUNCIATION

fee-neerr; gah-rah*ng*-teerr; shwah-zeerr; groh-seerr;
may-greerr; rah*ng*-pleerr; ray-ü-seerr; fee-nee; fee-nee;
fee-nee; fee-nee-so*ng*; fee-nee-say; fee-neess;
rah-porr; or-deen-ah-tuhr; por-tah-bluh; gah-toh; vairr;
o-kahz-yo*ng*; say-zeerr

Exercise 1

Translate:

1. I am finishing the report.
2. We guarantee the laptop.
3. She chooses a cake.
4. He is putting on weight.
5. They (f.) are losing weight.
6. They (m.) are filling the glasses.
7. We seize the opportunity.

3.2 DEMONSTRATIVES: THIS, THAT, THESE, THOSE

Both "this" and "that" are expressed by:

ce (m. sing.)	**ce train**	this/that train
cette (f. sing.)	**cette voiture**	this/that car

ce becomes **cet** before a vowel or h: **cet hélicoptère**

Both "these" and "those" are expressed by:

ces (m. and f. pl.) **ces avions**   these/those planes

If a distinction needs to be made between "this" and "that" or "these" and "those," you can add **-ci** (short for **ici** "here") or **-là** ("there") to the noun:
ce train-ci   this train
ce train-là   that train

VOCABULARY 2

le guichet	ticket office
l'ascenseur (m.)	elevator (lift)
le compartiment	compartment
le billet	ticket
la gare	railway station
la place	seat
rapide	fast
important	important
fermé	closed
cher, chère (f.)	expensive
plein	full
réservé	reserved
occupé	occupied
valable	valid

IMITATED PRONUNCIATION

suh tra*ng*; set ay-lee-kop-tairr; set vwah-türr; say zahv-yo*ng*; gee-shay; ah-sah*ng*-suhr; ko*ng*-pahr-tee-mah*ng*; bee-yay; gahr; plahs; rah-peed; a*ng*-por-tah*ng*; fairr-may; shairr; pla*ng*; ray-zairr-vay; o-kü-pay; vah-lahbluh

Exercise 2

Translate:

1. This train is fast.
2. This railway station is important.
3. This ticket office is closed.
4. That car is expensive.
5. That elevator is full.
6. These seats are reserved.
7. These compartments are occupied.
8. Those tickets are valid.

3.3 USEFUL EXPRESSIONS USING **AVOIR**

In French, there are a number of expressions with **avoir** "to have" that would be expressed in English with the verb "to be":

avoir faim	to be hungry
avoir soif	to be thirsty
avoir chaud	to be warm
avoir froid	to be cold
avoir raison	to be right
avoir tort	to be wrong

avoir is also used in connection with age:

Il a douze ans. He is twelve. (lit. "He has twelve years.")

IMITATED PRONUNCIATION

ah-vwahr fa*ng*; swahf; shoh; frwah; ray-zo*ng*; torr; ah*ng*

Exercise 3

Give the opposite of:

1. Il a raison.
2. Elle a chaud.
3. Ils ont tort.
4. Elles ont froid.

3.4 MORE NEGATIVES: NEVER, NOTHING, ETC.

We've already seen that "not" is expressed by putting **ne (n')** before the verb and **pas** after:

Je ne travaille pas. I don't work.
Il n'écoute pas. He isn't listening.

Here are some more negatives and model sentences:

ne ... jamais	never
ne ... rien	nothing, not anything
ne ... personne	no one, not anyone
ne ... plus	no longer, not anymore

Il ne travaille jamais. He never works.
Elle n'exporte rien. She doesn't export anything.
Ils n'invitent personne. They don't invite anyone.
Je ne fume plus. I don't smoke anymore.

NOTE:
Rien and **personne** can also begin a sentence:

Rien n'est cher. Nothing is expensive.
Personne ne fume ici. No one smokes here.

After a negative, **un, une, du, de la, de l', des** change to **de (d')**:

Je mange de la salade. I eat salad.
Je ne mange jamais de salade. I never eat salad.

VOCABULARY 3

le fromage	cheese
l'homme/la femme d'affaires	businessperson
la glace	ice cream
le/la diététicien/-ienne	dietician
manger	to eat
rencontrer	to meet
en	in, by

IMITATED PRONUNCIATION

nuh; zhah-may; ree-a*ng*; pairr-sonn; plü; fro-mahzh;
  om/fam dah-fairr; glahs; dyay-tay-tees-ya*ng*/yen;
mah*ng*-zhay; rah*ng*-ko*ng*-tray; ah*ng*

Exercise 4

Answer the questions using "not," as follows:

Vous voyagez en voiture?   Do you travel by car?
Non, je ne voyage pas en voiture.   No, I don't travel
by car.

1. Vous travaillez?
2. Vous écoutez?
3. Vous avez faim?

Now answer using "never":

4. Est-ce que vous choisissez du fromage?
5. Est-ce que vous téléphonez?
6. Est-ce que vous avez froid?

Now answer using "nothing":

7. Mange-t-il une glace?
8. Prépare-t-elle un rapport?
9. Exporte-t-il des imprimantes?

Now answer using "no one":

10. Nous invitons des hommes d'affaires?

11. Nous choisissons Paul?

12. Nous rencontrons la diététicienne?

Now answer using "no longer":

13. Est-ce qu'ils ont une voiture?

14. Est-ce qu'elles habitent à Paris?

15. Est-ce qu'elles travaillent?

3.5 ASKING WHERE?, WHEN?, HOW?, ETC.

Here are some words for asking questions in French:

où? where?
Où est-ce que vous habitez? Where do you live?

quand? when?
Quand écoutez-vous la radio?
When do you listen to the radio?

comment? how?
Comment allez-vous?
How are you? (literally: How do you go?)

qui? who? whom?
Qui parle français? Who speaks French?
Qui est-ce qu'elle invite? Whom is she inviting?

pourquoi? why?
Pourquoi téléphone-t-elle?
Why is she telephoning?

Note the reply to **pourquoi** is **parce que** "because."

quel (m.), **quelle** (f.)
quels (m. pl.), **quelles** (f. pl.) which (what)?

Quelle chambre réservons-nous?
Which room are we reserving?

combien? how much? how many?
Combien coûte ce livre?
How much does this book cost?
Combien de fromage désirez-vous?
How much cheese do you want?
Combien de trains y a-t-il?
How many trains are there?

Note: **combien** takes **de (d')** when followed by a noun.

que (**qu'** before a vowel) or **qu'est-ce que** what?
Que mangez-vous? or **Qu'est-ce que vous mangez?**
What are you eating?

Note the word order in the above two questions.

VOCABULARY 4	
le film	film
le soir	evening
l'euro (m.)	euro
l'allemand (m.)	German
l'espagnol (m.)	Spanish
bien	well
merci	thank you
chercher	to look for

IMITATED PRONUNCIATION

oo; kahng; ko-mah*ng*; ko-mah*ng* tah-lay voo; kee; poorr-
kwah; pahr-skuh; kel; ko*ng*-bee-a*ng*; koot; lee-vruh; day-
zee-ray voo; yah-teel; kuh; kess-kuh; mah*ng*-zhay; feelm;
swahr; ürroh; ahl-mah*ng*; ess-pan-yol; bee-a*ng*; mairr-
see; shairr-shay

Exercise 5

Below are 10 replies. What were the questions?
The important words are printed in italics.

1. Je travaille *à Paris.*
2. Je regarde le film *ce soir.*
3. *Bien,* merci.
4. *Pierre* téléphone.
5. Ils cherchent *Nicole.*
6. Parce que *j'ai faim.*
7. Je parle *espagnol et allemand.*
8. J'ai *quatre* livres.
9. Ce journal coûte *trois euros.*
10. J'exporte *des voitures.*

3

3.6 THE IMPERATIVE: GIVING ORDERS

On occasion, you may need to ask or tell people to do
things. Simply omit the **vous, tu,** or **nous** from the
present tense:

Téléphonez.	Telephone.
Choisissez.	Choose.
Invitons Paul.	Let's invite Paul.
Ne téléphonez pas.	Don't telephone.
N'invitons pas Paul.	Let's not invite Paul.

NOTE: the final **s** of **-er** verbs is dropped in the familiar
singular imperative:

Choisis.	Choose.
Finis.	Finish.
Téléphone.	Telephone.

To soften the tone, you can add **s'il vous plaît** or **s'il te
plaît** (fam. sing.), meaning "please," to the imperative.

VOCABULARY 5

les bagages (m.)	luggage
la méthode	method
trop	too much, too many
monter	to bring up, to take up
acheter	to buy

NOTE: **acheter** has a grave accent in the singular and third-person plural, which affects the pronunciation. See section 12.5.

j'achète	**nous achetons**
tu achètes	**vous achetez**
il/elle achète	**ils/elles achètent**

IMITATED PRONUNCIATION

bah-gahzh; may-tod; troh; mo*ng*-tay; ahsh-tay;
zhah-shet; tü ah-shet; eel ah-shet; el ah-shet;
noo zahsh-to*ng*; voo zahsh-tay; eel zah-shet; el zah-shet

Exercise 6

Tell your friend …

1. … to reserve two rooms.
2. … to look for François.
3. … to seize the opportunity.
4. … to choose the Hugo method.
5. … to take up the luggage.
6. … not to buy too much.
7. … not to finish the ice cream.
8. … not to smoke.

And now make some suggestions:

9. Let's speak French.
10. Let's listen to the radio.
11. Let's finish the report.

le régime	diet
le sport	sports, exercise
la chose	thing
la vie	life
penser	to think
je pense que	I think that
je dois	I must
faire	to do
(vous faites)	(you do)
raccourcir	to shorten
chaque	each
certain	certain
bien	good, fine (as an adverb)
complètement	completely
régulièrement	regularly
toujours	always
entre	for, between
pour	in order to
bonjour	good morning, good afternoon

3

IMITATED PRONUNCIATION

ray-zheem; sporr; shohz; vee; pah*ng*-say; zhuh pah*ng*s kuh; zhuh dwah; fairr; voo fet; rah-koor-seerr; shahk; sairr-ta*ng*; bee-a*ng*; ko*ng*-plet-mah*ng*; ray-gül-yairr-mah*ng*; too-zhoorr; ah*ng*truh; poorr; bo*ng*-zhoorr

3

Un dialogue entre un homme d'affaires et une diététicienne

HOMME D'AFFAIRES **Bonjour, madame.**
DIÉTÉTICIENNE **Bonjour, monsieur. Un petit instant, s'il vous plaît, je finis ce rapport. Bon. Comment allez-vous?**
HOMME D'AFFAIRES **Je pense que je grossis.**
DIÉTÉTICIENNE **Ah? Vous ne réussissez pas à maigrir? Pourquoi pas?**
HOMME D'AFFAIRES **J'ai toujours faim. J'ai toujours soif. Qu'est-ce que je dois faire?**
DIÉTÉTICIENNE **Faites du sport régulièrement. Saisissez chaque occasion pour manger de la salade.**
HOMME D'AFFAIRES **Et qu'est-ce que je ne dois pas faire?**
DIÉTÉTICIENNE **Ne choisissez jamais de gâteaux. Ne choisissez jamais de glaces. Ne choisissez jamais de fromage.**
HOMME D'AFFAIRES **Très bien. Et pour le vin?**
DIÉTÉTICIENNE **Ne remplissez jamais votre verre complètement.**
HOMME D'AFFAIRES **Vous me garantissez ce régime?**
DIÉTÉTICIENNE **Oui. Une chose est certaine: si vous grossissez, vous raccourcissez votre vie.**
HOMME D'AFFAIRES **Oui, madame. Vous avez raison.**

TRANSLATION

A dialogue between a businessman and a dietician

BUSINESSMAN	Good morning (madam).
DIETICIAN	Good morning (sir). One moment, please, I'm just finishing [literally "I finish"] this report. Good. How are you?
BUSINESSMAN	I think I'm putting on weight.
DIETICIAN	Oh? You're not managing to lose weight [literally "slim"]? Why not?
BUSINESSMAN	I'm always hungry. I'm always thirsty. What should I do?
DIETICIAN	Do some exercise regularly. Eat salad whenever you can. [Literally "Seize every opportunity to eat salad."]
BUSINESSMAN	And what shouldn't I do?
DIETICIAN	Never choose cakes. Never choose ice cream. Never choose cheese.
BUSINESSMAN	Fine. And what about wine?
DIETICIAN	Never fill your glass completely.
BUSINESSMAN	Do you vouch for this diet?
DIETICIAN	Yes. One thing's certain: if you put on weight, you shorten your life.
BUSINESSMAN	Yes (madam). You're right.

3

Week 4

- The present perfect tense (used to talk about the past), in both its affirmative and negative forms
- Possessive adjectives ("my," "your," "his," etc.)
- The expression **c'est** ("it is")
- Expressing the time
- An important irregular verb, **partir** ("to leave")
- More numbers
- Seasons, months, dates, and days of the week
- The position of adjectives (before/after the noun)

4 | 4.1 THE PRESENT PERFECT

The French present perfect tense can translate to various forms of the English past: "I have talked" or "I talked." As in English, the French perfect tenses are usually (though not always) formed with **avoir** (to have) and a past participle (the -ed form of a verb, e.g. talked): **j'ai parlé**.

To form the past participle in French:

replace the **-er** ending of the infinitive with **-é**

replace the **-ir** ending of the infinitive with **-i**

Verbs ending in **-er**	Verbs ending in **-ir**
j'ai parlé	**j'ai fini**
tu as preparé	**tu as garanti**
il a habité	**il a choisi**
elle a travaillé	**elle a grossi**
nous avons regardé	**nous avons maigri**
vous avez écouté	**vous avez saisi**
ils ont voyagé	**ils ont raccourci**
elles ont téléphoné	**elles ont rempli**

VOCABULARY 1

le document	document
l'Italie (f.)	Italy
la Manche	(English) Channel

copier	to copy
dépenser	to spend (money)
passer	to spend (time)
traverser	to cross

IMITATED PRONUNCIATION

pahr-lay; pray-pah-ray; ah-bee-tay; fee-nee;
gah-rah*ng*-tee; shwah-zee; do-kü-mah*ng*;
ee-tah-lee; mah*ng*sh; kop-yay; day-pah*ng*-say;
pah-say; trah-vairr-say

4

Exercise 1

◀×

Translate:

1. I have lived in France.
2. I have worked in Italy.
3. I have reserved the rooms.
4. She listened to the radio.
5. She watched the television.
6. She prepared the report.
7. He has put on weight.
8. He has chosen the cheese.
9. He has finished the book.
10. We copied the document.
11. We bought the car.
12. We telephoned.
13. You guaranteed the laptop.
14. You seized the opportunity.
15. You invited the president.
16. They (m.) have lost weight.
17. They (f.) have spent 15 euros.
18. They (f.) have crossed the Channel.

You may also need to say what you haven't done:

je n'ai pas copié
tu n'as pas traversé
il n'a pas passé
elle n'a pas acheté
nous n'avons pas invité
vous n'avez pas garanti
ils n'ont pas rempli
elles n'ont pas fini

Note the position of **pas** every time.

Exercise 2

Answer the questions as follows:
Avez-vous travaillé en Italie?
Have you worked in Italy?
Non, je n'ai pas travaillé en Italie.
No, I haven't worked in Italy.

1. Avez-vous réservé la chambre?
2. Avez-vous écouté la radio?
3. A-t-il regardé le film?
4. A-t-elle préparé le document?
5. Est-ce que nous avons fini?
6. Est-ce qu'ils ont choisi?
7. Est-ce qu'elles ont mangé?

4.3 POSSESSIVES: MY, YOUR, HIS, HER, ETC.

It is important to be able to establish ownership:

	m. sing.	f. sing.	m. and f. pl.
my	mon	ma	mes
your (fam.)	ton	ta	tes
his/her/its	son	sa	ses
our	notre	notre	nos
your	votre	votre	vos
their	leur	leur	leurs

Note that these adjectives agree with the thing possessed, not with the possessor:

ma femme	my wife
son mari	her husband
sa chambre	his or her bedroom
ses clés	his or her keys

However, note also that if the following noun begins with a vowel, **mon, ton, son** are used instead of **ma, ta, sa,** even if the noun is feminine:

mon amie	my friend (f.)
ton agence	your agency
son enquête	his/her survey

To the French ear, this allows for a more flowing liaison between words (see the pronunciation section).

VOCABULARY 2

le vol	flight
l'horaire (m.)	timetable
la ceinture de sécurité	seat belt
la place	seat
attacher	to fasten, to attach
premier, première (f.)	first

IMITATED PRONUNCIATION

mo*ng*; mah; may; to*ng*; tah; tay; so*ng*; sah; say; notruh;
noh; votruh; voh; luhr; fahm; mah-ree; vol; o-rairr;
sa*ng*-tür duh say-kü-ree-tay; plahs; ah-tah-shay;
pruhm-yay; prerm-yairr

Exercise 3

Translate:

1. Your first flight.
2. Fasten your seat belt.
3. Where are our tickets?
4. Here is her passport.
5. Here is his seat.
6. Their suitcases are in the plane.
7. Where are my newspapers?

4.4 THE EXPRESSION **C'EST** ("IT IS")

C'est facile.	It is easy.
C'est difficile.	It is difficult.
C'est très important.	It is very important.
C'est moins cher.	It is less expensive.

VOCABULARY 3

possible	possible
impossible	impossible
magnifique	wonderful
affreux	dreadful
tôt	early
tard	late

IMITATED PRONUNCIATION

say; mwah*ng*; po-seebluh; a*ng*-po-seebluh; mahn-yee-feek; ah-fruh; toh; tahr

Exercise 4

Give the opposite of:

1. C'est intéressant.
2. C'est bon.
3. C'est possible.
4. C'est facile.
5. C'est magnifique.
6. C'est tard.

4.5 THE TIME

If you intend to keep appointments, catch trains and buses, and so on, you need to be familiar with the way in which the time is expressed in French:

Quelle heure est-il? What time is it?
Il est une heure. It is one o'clock.
Il est deux heures. It is two o'clock.
Il est trois heures. It is three o'clock.
Il est quatre heures. It is four o'clock.
Il est midi. It is midday.
Il est minuit. It is midnight.

Il est cinq heures et quart. It is a quarter past five.
Il est cinq heures et demie. It is half past five.
Il est six heures moins le quart. It is a quarter to six.

Il est six heures dix. It is ten past six.
Il est sept heures moins cinq. It is five to seven.

À quelle heure? At what time?
À huit heures. At eight o'clock.

À neuf heures du matin.
At nine in the morning.
À neuf heures du soir.
At nine in the evening.
À deux heures de l'après-midi.
At two in the afternoon.

VOCABULARY 4

le car	coach
le bateau	boat
l'avion (m.)	airplane
la conférence de presse	press conference
arriver	to arrive

IRREGULAR VERB

partir (to leave)

Present tense
je pars
tu pars
il/elle part
nous partons
vous partez
ils/elles partent

IMITATED PRONUNCIATION

kel uhr ay teel; eel ay ün uhr; eel ay duh zuhr; trwah zuhr;
mee-dee; meen-wee; kahr; duh-mee; ah kel uhr; ah nuh
vuhr dü mah-ta*ng*; dü swahr; duh lah-pray-mee-dee;
kahr; bah-toh; ah-vyo*ng*; ko*ng*-fay-rah*ng*ss duh press;
ah-ree-vay; pahr-teerr; pahr; pahr-to*ng*; pahr-tay; pahrt

Exercise 5

Add 15 minutes to the time stated:

1. Il est deux heures.
2. Il est quatre heures et quart.
3. Il est six heures moins le quart.
4. Il est huit heures cinq.
5. Le train arrive à dix heures.
6. Le car arrive à onze heures et demie.
7. Le bateau part à midi dix.
8. L'avion part à minuit et demi.*
9. La présidente arrive à neuf heures.
10. La conférence de presse est à dix heures.

*"Demi" is the masc. adj. to agree with "minuit" (m.);
use the fem. form "demie" to agree with "heure" (f.).

4.6 MORE NUMBERS

Here are some more numbers:

16	seize	33	trente-trois
17	dix-sept	40	quarante
18	dix-huit	41	quarante et un
19	dix-neuf	42	quarante-deux
20	vingt	50	cinquante
21	vingt et un	51	cinquante et un
22	vingt-deux	52	cinquante-deux
23	vingt-trois	60	soixante
30	trente	61	soixante et un
31	trente et un	62	soixante-deux
32	trente-deux		

IMITATED PRONUNCIATION

sez; dee-set; deez-weet; deez-nuhf; vang; vang-tay-ung;
vangt-duh; vangt-trwah; trahngt; kah-rahngt; sang-kahngt;
swah-sahngt

4.7 SEASONS OF THE YEAR

le printemps	spring
l'été (m.)	summer
l'automne (m.)	autumn (fall)
l'hiver (m.)	winter

The seasons are all masculine.

en été	in summer
en automne	in autumn (fall)
en hiver	in winter
but	
au printemps	in spring

4.8 MONTHS OF THE YEAR

janvier	January
février	February
mars	March
avril	April
mai	May
juin	June
juillet	July
août	August
septembre	September
octobre	October
novembre	November
décembre	December

Note that the months of the year are not written with a capital letter in French.

IMITATED PRONUNCIATION

luh pra*ng*-tah*ng*; lay-tay; loh-ton; lee-vairr; zhah*ng*v-yay; fayvr-yay; mahrss; ah-vreel; may; zhwa*ng*; zhwee-yay; oot; sep-tah*ng*bruh; ok-tobruh; no-vah*ng*bruh; day-sah*ng*bruh

4.9 DATES

Quelle date sommes-nous aujourd'hui?
What is the date today?
Nous sommes le deux janvier.
It's the 2nd of January.
Nous sommes le huit février.
It's the 8th of February.
Nous sommes le quinze mars.
It's the 15th of March.
Nous sommes le vingt avril.
It's the 20th of April.
Nous sommes le trente mai.
It's the 30th of May.

Note for the first of each month in French, it's
le premier:

le premier juin the 1st of June
le premier juillet the 1st of July
but
le vingt et un août the 21st ("21") of August
le trente et un octobre the 31st ("31") of October

Note also how you say "in" a certain month:

en août in August
en septembre in September
en octobre in October
en novembre in November

Exercise 6

Write in full the following dates:

1. New Year's Day
2. May Day
3. the storming of the Bastille (July 14)
4. Christmas Day
5. Armistice Day (November 11)
6. The first day of spring (March 21)

4

4.10 DAYS OF THE WEEK

lundi	Monday
mardi	Tuesday
mercredi	Wednesday
jeudi	Thursday
vendredi	Friday
samedi	Saturday
dimanche	Sunday

Note that the days of the week are not written with a capital letter in French.

Avez-vous travaillé lundi?
Did you work on Monday?
Pierre téléphone jeudi.
Pierre will telephone (lit. "is telephoning") on Thursday.
Pierre téléphone le jeudi.
Pierre telephones on Thursdays.

Note in these examples that the preposition "on" is omitted in French. In the last example, **le** indicates that the action takes place regularly.

IMITATED PRONUNCIATION

daht; oh-zhoor-dwee; lung-dee; mahr-dee;
mairr-kruh-dee; zhuh-dee; vahng-druh-dee;
sahm-dee; dee-mahngsh

Exercise 7

Translate:

1. I worked on Monday.
2. I listened to the radio on Tuesday.
3. I watched television on Wednesday.
4. I finished the report on Thursday.
5. I bought a book on Friday.
6. I telephoned my wife on Saturday.
7. I spoke Spanish on Sunday.
8. I work on Mondays.
9. She listens to the radio on Tuesdays.
10. We watch television on Wednesdays.

4

4.11 THE POSITION OF ADJECTIVES

In French, adjectives are usually placed after the noun:

un livre difficile a difficult book
un médecin français a French doctor
une voiture américaine an American car
une langue importante an important language

But the following adjectives normally precede the noun:

bon, bonne (f.)	good
mauvais	bad
petit	small
grand	large
joli	pretty
jeune	young
vieux (m. sing. and pl.)	old
vieil (m. sing. before a vowel or h)	
vieille (f.)	
vieilles (f. pl.)	
nouveau (m. sing.)	new
nouvel (m. sing before a vowel or h)	
nouvelle (f.)	
nouveaux (m. pl.)	
nouvelles (f. pl.)	

Examples:
un bon employé a good employee
une jeune pilote a young pilot (f.)
un vieil ordinateur an old computer
un nouvel appareil-photo a new camera
un mauvais client a bad client
une jolie fleur a pretty flower

IMITATED PRONUNCIATION

zho-lee; zhuhn; vyuh; vyay'ee; noo-voh; noo-vel;
ah*ng*-plwah-yay; klee-yah*ng*; fluhr

Londres (m.)	London
l'argent (m.)	money
le départ	departure
la conversation	conversation
la semaine	week
les vacances (f.)	vacations
la nourriture	food
la chaleur	heat
visiter	to visit
trouver	to find
consulter	to consult
il faut	one must, it is necessary to
indigeste	indigestible
insupportable	unbearable
moi	me (see section 8.4)
un peu	a little
à l'avance	in advance
des (de + les = des)	of the
d'accord	okay, fine
le retour	return

IMITATED PRONUNCIATION

longdruh; ahr-zhahng; day-pahr; kong-vairr-sah-see-ong;
suh-men; vah-kahngss; noo-ree-türr; shah-luhr;
vee-zee-tay; troo-vay; kong-sül-tay; eel foh;
ang-dee-zhest; ang-sü-porr-tahbluh; mwah; ung puh;
ah lah-vahngss; day; dakor; ruh-toor

CONVERSATION

À une agence de voyages à Londres

Une conversation entre un employé français et une cliente américaine qui habite à Londres. La cliente saisit l'occasion pour parler français.

CLIENTE **Mon mari et moi, nous désirons passer deux semaines en France au printemps. Nous avons visité l'Italie en août, mais nous n'avons pas passé de bonnes vacances.**

EMPLOYÉ **Ah? Pourquoi?**

CLIENTE **Nous avons trouvé la nourriture un peu indigeste, nous avons trouvé la chaleur insupportable, et nous avons dépensé beaucoup d'argent.**

EMPLOYÉ **Avez-vous l'intention de voyager en avion?**

CLIENTE **Non, par le train, c'est plus agréable.**

EMPLOYÉ **Un petit instant, madame. Je consulte l'horaire de l'Eurostar. Il y a des départs à huit heures, à neuf heures, à dix heures, à onze heures, etc. Il faut réserver les places à l'avance.**

CLIENTE **Oui, d'accord. Départ le 9 avril, retour le 23 avril.**

EMPLOYÉ **Un instant, s'il vous plaît.**

At a travel agency in London

A conversation between a French travel representative and an American customer who lives in London. The customer seizes the opportunity to speak French.

4

CUSTOMER   My husband and I want to spend two weeks in France in the spring. We visited Italy in August, but we didn't have a good vacation.

AGENT   Oh? Why not?

CUSTOMER   We found the food a little heavy [literally "indigestible"], we found the heat unbearable, and we spent a lot of money.

AGENT   Do you intend to travel by plane?

CUSTOMER   No, by train, it's more pleasant.

AGENT   Just one moment, madam. I'll consult the Eurostar timetable. There are departures at eight o'clock, at nine o'clock, at ten o'clock, at eleven o'clock, etc. You need to reserve seats in advance.

CUSTOMER   Yes, okay. Departure on April 9, return on April 23.

AGENT   One moment, please.

Self-assessment test 1 A–C

This self-assessment test, based on weeks 1–4, will allow you to check your progress and see whether you need to review anything. Deduct one point for every grammatical mistake or wrong spelling. The answers and score assessment are in the key.

A. Nouns   Total: 8 points
Give the French for:

1. the doctor
2. the computer
3. some wine
4. some beer
5. my car
6. my keys
7. this train
8. these newspapers

B. Adjectives   Total: 5 points
Give the opposite of:

1. pauvre
2. malheureux
3. intéressant
4. magnifique
5. facile

C. Verbs   Total: 10 points
Which French verb do you associate with the following?

1. la télévision
2. la radio
3. la méthode Hugo
4. un sport
5. la ceinture de sécurité
6. une chambre d'hôtel
7. une agence de voyages
8. l'occasion pour parler français
9. l'horaire des trains
10. la Manche

Self-assessment test 1 D–H

D. The time   Total: 8 points

Add 15 minutes to the time mentioned:

1. Le train part à six heures.
2. Le car part à huit heures et demie.
3. Le Président arrive à dix heures cinq.
4. La conférence de presse est à onze heures et demie.

E. Days of the week   Total: 4 points

Write down the day before the one shown:

1. jeudi   **3.** samedi
2. lundi   **4.** mercredi

F. Total: 4 points

What difference in meaning is there between "jeudi" and "le jeudi"?

G. Months of the year   Total: 4 points

Write down the date a month after the one shown:

1. le deux janvier
2. le cinq mars
3. le douze mai
4. le trente et un juillet

H. The present perfect   Total: 8 points

It all happened on Monday! Answer these questions in the present perfect, as in this example:

Q: Avez-vous l'intention de regarder le film?
A: Non, j'ai regardé le film lundi.

1. Avez-vous l'intention de réserver les chambres?
2. A-t-il l'intention de finir le livre?
3. A-t-elle l'intention de photocopier le document?
4. Ont-ils l'intention de téléphoner?

4

Self-assessment test 1 I–L

I. The present perfect (negative)   Total: 16 points
Give the French for:

1. I haven't finished the report.
2. She didn't phone her husband on Saturday.
3. We haven't visited Italy.
4. They (m.) haven't lost weight.

J. Numbers   Total: 18 points
Complete the following, writing the totals in words:

a. 14 + 15   f. 30 + 20
b. 20 + 16   g. 10 + 5
c. 23 + 22   h. 30 + 32
d. 27 + 4   i. 14 + 2
e. 14 + 30

K. Do you remember …?   Total: 1 point
Which verb is used in French when talking about a person's age?

L. Conversation (role-play)   Total: 14 points
Play the part of the customer in this short scene:

CLIENTE   We want to spend two weeks in France in the spring. We visited Italy in August, but we found the heat unbearable.
EMPLOYÉ   Avez-vous l'intention de voyager en avion?
CLIENTE   No, by train, it's more pleasant.
EMPLOYÉ   Un petit instant, madame, je consulte l'horaire de l'Eurostar. Il faut réserver les places à l'avance.
CLIENTE   Yes, okay! Departure on April 9, return on April 23.

Week 5

- *Regular and irregular* **-re** *verbs, in both the present and present perfect tenses*
- *Introduction to adverbs*
- *The pronoun "it"*
- *Object pronouns ("me," "him," "her," "to him," "to her," etc.)*
- *Using object pronouns with the perfect tenses*
- *More irregular verbs, including the present perfect tense of* **être** *and* **avoir**

5.1 REGULAR VERBS ENDING IN -RE

A number of key verbs have an infinitive ending in **-re**:

vendre	to sell
rendre	to give back
attendre	to wait (for)
entendre	to hear
descendre	to go down/take down/bring down
répondre	to reply
perdre	to lose

The present tense is formed by removing the **-re** from the infinitive and adding the endings:

je	-s	nous	-ons
tu	-s	vous	-ez
il/elle	-	ils/elles	-ent

je vends	**nous vendons**
tu vends	**vous vendez**
il/elle vend	**ils/elles vendent**

The present perfect tense is formed by replacing the **-re** of the infinitive with **-u**:

j'ai vendu	**nous avons vendu**
tu as vendu	**vous avez vendu**
il/elle a vendu	**ils/elles ont vendu**

VOCABULARY 1

les parents (m.)	parents
le frère/la sœur	brother/sister
la musique	music
la maison	house
le père/la mère	father/mother
cela	that
dépendre de	to depend on
défendre	to defend, to forbid

IMITATED PRONUNCIATION

vahngdruh; rahngdruh; ah-tahngdruh; ahng-tahngdruh; day-sahngdruh; ray-pongdruh; pairrdruh; vahng; vahng-dong; vahng-day; vahngd; vahng-dü; pah-rahng; frairr; suhr; mü-zeek; may-zong; pairr; mairr; suh-lah; day-pahngdruh duh; day-fahngdruh

Exercise 1

Translate:

1. I am selling my car.
2. He is waiting for his wife.
3. We give back 60 euros.
4. That depends on my parents.
5. Do they (f.) hear the music?
6. She has sold her house.
7. We have not replied.
8. Have you brought down the luggage?
9. Are you (fam. sing.) waiting for your brother?
10. Have you (fam. sing.) lost your mother?

5.2 ■ IRREGULAR VERBS ENDING IN -RE

The following **-re** verbs are irregular, taking a slightly different pattern in the present tense and a very different pattern in the present perfect tense:

prendre	to take	**comprendre**	to understand
apprendre	to learn	**surprendre**	to surprise

<u>Present</u>
je prends   I take (or I am taking)
tu prends
il/elle prend
nous prenons
vous prenez
ils/elles prennent

<u>Present perfect</u>
j'ai pris	I took (or I have taken)
j'ai appris	I learned (have learned)
j'ai compris	I understood (have understood)
j'ai surpris	I surprised (have surprised)

IMITATED PRONUNCIATION

prahngdruh; ah-prah*ng*druh; ko*ng*-prah*ng*druh; sür-prah*ng*druh; prah*ng*; pruh-no*ng*; pruh-nay; pren; pree; ah-pree; ko*ng*-pree; sür-pree

Exercise 2

Change the present to the past and vice versa:

1. Est-ce que vous prenez le train?
2. J'apprends le français.
3. Avez-vous appris la langue?
4. Avez-vous compris?
5. Tu surprends souvent ton professeur?

The following irregular **-re** verbs have a similar pattern to that of the **prendre** group, but the consonant is doubled in the **nous**, **vous**, and **ils/elles** forms:

mettre	to put
permettre	to permit, to allow
promettre	to promise
soumettre	to submit

Present

je mets	I put (or I am putting)
tu mets	
il/elle met	
nous mettons	
vous mettez	
ils/elles mettent	

Present perfect

vous avez mis	you put (or have put)
vous avez permis	you (have) permitted
vous avez promis	you (have) promised
vous avez soumis	you (have) submitted

VOCABULARY 2

le matin	morning
le dictionnaire	dictionary
le projet	project, plan
l'enfant (m. and f.)	child
l'annonce (f.)	advertisement
la lettre	letter
permettre de	to allow to
promettre de	to promise to
rentrer	to return
tôt	early
tard	late
déjà	already

Note the construction with **défendre** and **permettre**:

Je défends à Paul de parler. I forbid Paul to speak.
Je permets à Paul de parler. I allow Paul to speak.

IMITATED PRONUNCIATION

metruh; pairr-metruh; pro-metruh; soo-metruh; may;
met-o*ng*; met-ay; met; mee; pairr-mee; pro-mee; soo-
mee; mah-ta*ng*; deeks-yo-nairr; pro-zhay; ah*ng*-fah*ng*;
ah-no*ng*s; letruh; rah*ng*-tray; toh; tahr; day-zhah

Exercise 3

Change the present to the past and vice versa:

1. Je mets une annonce dans le journal.
2. Il permet à son employé de partir tôt.
3. Vous promettez de répondre à la lettre?
4. Elle soumet le rapport ce matin.
5. Avez-vous mis le livre dans la valise?
6. Ont-ils permis à leurs enfants de rentrer tard?
7. Nous avons promis de parler français.
8. Avez-vous déjà soumis le projet?

5

5.4 ADVERBS: SAYING HOW THINGS ARE DONE

We often need to describe how things are done, for
example: rapidly, admirably, carefully.

In French, adverbs are formed by adding **-ment** to the
adjective, which is the equivalent of -ly in English:

rapide (rapid) becomes **rapidement** (rapidly)
admirable becomes **admirablement**
rare becomes **rarement**

If the adjective ends in a consonant, e.g. **malheureux**
(unfortunate), **-ment** is added to the feminine form:

immédiat	**immédiate** (f.)	**immédiatement**
général	**générale** (f.)	**généralement**
malheureux	**malheureuse** (f.)	**malheureusement**

VOCABULARY 3

attentif, attentive (f.)	careful
complet, complète (f.)	complete
lent	slow
normal	normal
principal	main
temporaire	temporary

IMITATED PRONUNCIATION

rah-peed; rah-peed-mah*ng*; ahd-mee-rahbluh;
ahd-mee-rah-bluh-mah*ng*; rahr; rahr-mahng;
ee-mayd-yaht-mah*ng*; zhay-nay-rahl-mah*ng*;
mah-luhr-ruhz-mah*ng*; ah-tah*ng*-teef; ah-tah*ng*-teev;
ko*ng*-play; ko*ng*-plet; lah*ng*; norr-mahl; pra*ng*-see-pahl;
tah*ng*-po-rairr

Exercise 4

Form adverbs from the following adjectives:

1. rapide

2. facile

3. final

4. heureux

5. attentif

6. lent

7. complet

8. normal

9. principal

10. temporaire

When "it" refers to something that has just been mentioned, the same word is used in French as for "he" or "she," depending on the gender of the noun:

Le vin? Il est très bon. The wine? It's very good.
La voiture? Elle est chère. The car? It's expensive.

Referring to things, "they" is expressed by **ils** or **elles**:

Les trains? Ils sont rapides.
The trains? They're fast.
Les places? Elles sont réservées.
The seats? They're reserved.

5

VOCABULARY 4

l'appareil (m.)	machine, device
le restaurant	restaurant
le produit	product
le message	message
le répondeur	answering machine
la poche	pocket
la qualité	quality
l'explication (f.)	explanation
clair	clear
en anglais	in English
excellent	excellent
interdire	to prohibit, to ban

IMITATED PRONUNCIATION

ah-pah-ray'ee; res-to-rah*ng*; pro-dwee; may-sahzh;
ray-po*ng*-duhr; pohsh; kah-lee-tay; eks-plee-kah-see-o*ng*;
klairr; ah*ng* nah*ng*-glay; ek-sel-ah*ng*; ah*ng*-tairr-deer

Exercise 5

Translate:

1. The report? It's very important.
2. The beer? It's bad.
3. The pocket? It's full.
4. The machine? It's excellent.
5. The restaurant? It's closed.
6. The quality? It's very good.
7. The products? They're French.
8. The messages? They're in English.
9. The explanation? It's not clear.
10. The mobile phone? It's not expensive.

5

5.6 OBJECT PRONOUNS: ME, HIM, HER, TO HIM, TO HER, IT, ETC.

Study the following:

Michel le rencontre Michel meets him
Michel la rencontre Michel meets her
Michel les rencontre Michel meets them
Hélène le vend (masc. object) Hélène sells it
Hélène la vend (fem. object) Hélène sells it
Paul nous félicite Paul congratulates us
Paul vous félicite Paul congratulates you
Sophie me choisit Sophie chooses me
Sophie te choisit Sophie chooses you
Sophie vous comprend Sophie understands you

The main things to notice are that:

• "Me," "him," "her," "us," "them," etc. come <u>before</u> the verb

• The words for "him," "her," "it," and "them" are just like the words for "the"

• The words for "us" and "you" are just like those for "we" and "you" (subject pronouns)

• "Me" in French is **me**; "you" (familiar singular) is **te**; "you" (plural) is **vous**

The object pronouns **me**, **nous**, **vous**, and **te** can also mean "to me," "to us," "to you":

il me parle he speaks to me
il nous répète he repeats to us
elle vous répond she replies to you
elle te vend she sells to you (fam.)

Both "to him" and "to her" are translated by **lui**:

je lui répète I repeat to him (or to her)

The plural "to them" is expressed by **leur**:

je leur parle I speak to them

Sometimes the "to" is not expressed in English, although clearly intended. Compare the French and the English:

Je lui vends la voiture. I sell him the car.
Nous leur téléphonons. We telephone them.

NOTE: **me**, **le**, **la**, and **te** become **m'**, **l'**, **t'** in front of a vowel or h: **il m'invite**; **elle l'écoute**; **je t'invite**

VOCABULARY 5

le client/la cliente	client, customer
le mode d'emploi	operating instructions
l'ami/l'amie	friend
la leçon	lesson
le commerçant/ la commerçante	shopkeeper
brancher	to plug in
mettre en marche	to start, to set going

klee-yah*ng*/yah*ng*t; mohd dah*ng*-plwah; ah-mee; luh-so*ng*; ko-mairr-sah*ng*/sah*ng*t; brah*ng*-shay; metruh ah*ng* mahrsh

Exercise 6

Answer the questions using pronouns, as follows:

Vous me comprenez? Do you understand me?

Oui, je vous comprends. Yes, I understand you.

1. Elle me cherche?
2. Elle vous consulte?
3. Vous rencontrez le client?
4. Vous photocopiez la leçon?
5. Il invite Nicole?
6. Il exporte les voitures?
7. Comprenons-nous le mode d'emploi?
8. Branchons-nous la radio?
9. Mettons-nous l'appareil en marche?
10. Photocopions-nous le document?
11. Elles nous répondent en français?
12. Ils téléphonent à Pierre?
13. Ils téléphonent à Nicole?
14. Ils téléphonent à Pierre et à Nicole?
15. Vous parlez à la commerçante?
16. Vous répondez à vos amis?
17. Vous permettez à vos enfants de rentrer tard?

5.7 DIRECT OBJECT PRONOUNS WITH THE PERFECT TENSES

When a direct object pronoun is used with the perfect tenses, the past participle of the verb has to agree in gender and number with the pronoun:

je l'ai invité	I invited him
je l'ai invitée	I invited her
je les ai invités	I invited them (men or men and women)
je les ai invitées	I invited them (women)

vous l'avez copié	you copied it **(le document)**
vous l'avez copiée	you copied it **(la leçon)**
vous les avez copiés	you copied them **(les documents)**
vous les avez copiées	you copied them **(les leçons)**
vous les avez copiés	you copied them **(les documents et les leçons)**

il m'a trouvé	he found me (man speaking)
il m'a trouvée	he found me (woman speaking)
il nous a trouvés	he found us (men speaking)
il nous a trouvées	he found us (women speaking)
il nous a trouvés	he found us (men and women speaking)

elle vous a consulté	she consulted you (m. doctor)
elle vous a consultée	she consulted you (f. doctor)
elle vous a consultés	she consulted you (m. doctors)
elle vous a consultées	she consulted you (f. doctors)
elle vous a consultés	she consulted you (m./f. doctors)

Note that this does NOT apply when the pronoun is an indirect object, meaning "to me," "to him," etc.

5

The pronunciation of all these endings is the same, i.e. "ay." However, when the past participle ends in a consonant—for example, **compris**—the addition of the feminine ending **-e** or **-es** results in this consonant being voiced rather than silent:

je l'ai comprise   I understood her
zhuh lay ko*ng*-preez

je les ai apprises I learned them (**les leçons**, for example)
zhe*r* lay zay ah-preez

Exercise 7

Answer the questions as follows:

Avez-vous rencontré le client? Did you meet the client?
Oui, je l'ai rencontré. Yes, I met him.

1. Avez-vous invité Pierre?
2. Avez-vous invité Nicole?
3. Avez-vous invité Pierre et Nicole?
4. A-t-il exporté les voitures?
5. A-t-elle consulté le médecin?
6. A-t-elle consulté la diététicienne?
7. A-t-elle consulté le médecin et la diététicienne?
8. Ont-ils branché la radio?
9. Ont-ils réservé les chambres?
10. Ont-ils perdu la clé?
11. Avons-nous compris le mode d'emploi?
12. Avons-nous compris la leçon?
13. Avons-nous compris les leçons?
14. Avons-nous compris les livres?
15. Avez-vous mis la clé dans votre poche?

5

VOCABULARY 6

l'appel téléphonique (m.)	telephone call
ici	here
tout	everything
même	even
depuis	since
peut-être	perhaps
il y a	ago
seul	single, only
utiliser	to use
aux (à + les = aux)	to the
répéter	to repeat

(See section 12.5 for how **répéter** slightly changes its spelling in the present tense.)

IRREGULAR VERBS

lire (to read)

Present tense

je lis	**nous lisons**
tu lis	**vous lisez**
il/elle lit	**ils/elles lisent**

Present perfect
j'ai lu, etc.

faire (to do, to make)

Present tense

je fais	**nous faisons**
tu fais	**vous faites**
il/elle fait	**ils/elles font**

Present perfect
j'ai fait, etc.

être (to be)	**avoir** (to have)
Present perfect	Present perfect
j'ai été, etc.	**j'ai eu**, etc.

IMITATED PRONUNCIATION

ah-pel tay-lay-fo-neek; ee-see; too; mem; duh-pwee; puh-tetruh; eel yah; suhl; ü-tee-lee-zay; oh; ray-pay-tay; zhuh lee; tü lee; eel lee; noo lee-zong; voo lee-zay; eel leez; zhay lü; fairr; zhuh fay; tü fay; eel fay; noo fuh-zong; voo fet; eel fong; zhay fay; etruh; zhay ay-tay; ah-vwahr; zhay ü

Une conversation entre une vendeuse et un client

CLIENT   **Bonjour, madame. Il y a deux semaines vous m'avez vendu un téléphone, mais il ne marche pas. Malheureusement, je ne reçois pas les appels téléphoniques de mes amis.**

VENDEUSE   **Je suis surprise d'apprendre cela, monsieur. Nos téléphones sont d'excellente qualité. Avez-vous lu le mode d'emploi?**

CLIENT   **Oui, je l'ai lu très attentivement. Attendez, je l'ai ici dans ma poche. Mais, où est-il? Je l'ai peut-être perdu.**

VENDEUSE   **Ce n'est pas grave, monsieur. Avez-vous branché l'appareil correctement? Avez-vous mis l'appareil en marche? Avez-vous compris les explications?**

CLIENT   **Oui, j'ai tout compris et j'ai tout fait correctement. J'ai même interdit à mes enfants de l'utiliser.**

VENDEUSE   **Permettez-moi de vous répéter, monsieur, que nos produits sont d'excellente qualité. Si vous n'avez pas reçu un seul appel depuis deux semaines, la seule explication possible, c'est que personne ne vous téléphone!**

5

A conversation between a sales assistant and a customer

CUSTOMER   Good morning. Two weeks ago, you sold me a telephone, but it doesn't work. Unfortunately, I'm not receiving my friends' telephone calls.

ASSISTANT   I'm surprised to hear [learn] that, sir. Our telephones are of excellent quality. Have you read the instruction booklet?

CUSTOMER   Yes, I read it very carefully. One moment [wait], I have it here in my pocket. But where is it? Perhaps I've lost it.

ASSISTANT   It doesn't matter. Did you plug the machine in correctly? Did you start the machine? Did you understand the instructions [explanations]?

CUSTOMER   Yes, I understood everything and I did everything correctly. I've even forbidden my children to use it.

ASSISTANT   Allow me to repeat, sir, that our products are of excellent quality. If you haven't received a single call for two weeks, the only possible explanation is that no one telephones you!

Week 6

- *Prepositions: "in," "to," "from," etc.*
- *The expression* **il y a** *("there is/are")*
- *The comparative and superlative of adjectives and adverbs, plus irregular forms ("good/better/best")*
- *Talking about the weather*
- *Verbs that form the past tense with* **être**
- *The expressions* **je voudrais** *("I would like") and* **il faut** *("it is necessary to")*

6.1 PREPOSITIONS: IN, TO, FROM, ETC.

Here are some useful French prepositions. Many of them are used to indicate position:

dans	in
en	in, into
sur	on
sous	under
devant	in front of
derrière	behind
près de	near
à côté de	next to
en face de	across from (opposite)
à	at, to
de	of, from
pour	for
avec	with
sans	without
après	after
avant	before

We've seen that in French, the article and certain prepositions form contractions: **à le** or **à les** become **au** or **aux**; **de le** and **de les** become **du** or **des**.

Examples:

au musée	at/to the museum
à la boulangerie	at/to the bakery
aux magasins	at/to the shops
du bureau de poste	of/from the post office

de la pharmacie	of/from the pharmacy (chemist)
des hôtels	of/from the hotels
dans la voiture	in the car
en France	in (or to) France
à côté de la boucherie	next to the butcher shop
en face de la poissonnerie	across from (opposite) the fishmonger's
près de l'épicerie	near the food shop
sur la table	on the table
sous la chaise	under the chair
devant l'hôpital	in front of the hospital
derrière l'université	behind the university
avec mon mari	with my husband
sans difficulté	without difficulty
après le petit déjeuner	after breakfast
avant le dîner	before dinner

NOTE: Both **dans** and **en** mean "in," but **dans** is more specific: **dans** is generally used before **le**, **la**, **les**, **un**, **une**, **mon**, **votre**, etc.; otherwise, **en** is used. Contrast:

dans la voiture de mon frère	in my brother's car
en voiture	(to go) by car
dans le sud de la France	in the south of France
en France	in France

Note also the following difference:

dans deux semaines in two weeks' time
(I'll begin the work **dans deux semaines**)

en deux semaines within two weeks
(I did the work **en deux semaines**)

6

6.2 IL Y A ("THERE IS/ARE")

We've already seen **il y a**, but let's look at this very useful expression more closely. Though it is formed from the verb **avoir**, it means "there is" or "there are." It is used with both singular and plural nouns:

Il y a un taxi devant l'hôtel.
There's a taxi in front of the hotel.
Il y a des journaux ici.
There are some newspapers here.
Est-ce qu'il y a une banque ici?
Is there a bank here?

VOCABULARY 1

le restaurant	restaurant
le supermarché	supermarket
le tunnel	tunnel
le numéro de téléphone	telephone number
le cinéma	cinema (movie theater)
le théâtre	theater
le spectacle	show, performance
l'ami(e)	friend
les États-Unis	United States
la serviette	napkin, towel
l'église (f.)	church
la librairie	bookstore
la bibliothèque	library
le chargeur de téléphone	phone charger
l'épicerie	small food shop, deli
c'est difficile de	it is difficult to
Angleterre	England

6

IRREGULAR VERBS

aller (to go)
Present tense
je vais
tu vas
il/elle va
nous allons
vous allez
ils/elles vont

venir (to come)
Present tense
je viens
tu viens
il/elle vient
nous venons
vous venez
ils/elles viennent

6

IMITATED PRONUNCIATION

You should now be feeling more confident as far as French pronunciation is concerned, so we won't provide the imitated pronunciation anymore. Continue using the audio in the app as you work through the course. Listening and repeating the words and sentences out loud is the best way to perfect your pronunciation.

Exercise 1

Translate:

1. There's a napkin on the table.
2. There's a taxi in front of the hotel.
3. There's a restaurant behind the church.
4. There's a supermarket next to the bank.
5. There's a bookstore across from the university.
6. Is there a bakery near the station?
7. Are there any English books in the library?
8. Is there a tunnel under the Channel?
9. I'm going to the cinema.
10. She's going to the United States.
11. Do you have the telephone number of the theater?
12. I have bought a newspaper for my friend.
13. She's learning French with some friends.
14. It's difficult to work without my laptop.
15. Let's eat after the show.
16. Let's telephone before 9 o'clock.

6

6.3 COMPARISON OF ADJECTIVES

In English, comparisons are made by adding "-er" to an adjective or by using "more" or "less." In French, you simply put **plus** (more) or **moins** (less) in front of the adjective:

Cet hôtel est grand.
This hotel is large.
Cet hôtel est plus grand.
This hotel is larger.
Cette lettre est importante.
This letter is important.
Cette lettre est plus importante.
This letter is more important.
Ce livre est moins difficile.
This book is less difficult.

The word "than" is expressed by **que**:

La cathédrale est plus belle que l'église.
The cathedral is more beautiful than the church.
Le film est moins intéressant que le livre.
The film is less interesting than the book.

Note also:

aussi ... que   as ... as
pas aussi ... que not ... as

Le car est aussi rapide que la voiture.
Going by coach is as fast as going by car.
Le train n'est pas aussi rapide que l'avion.
The train is not as fast as the plane.

6.4 COMPARISON OF ADVERBS

Adverbs follow the same pattern as adjectives:

Pierre travaille lentement.
Pierre works slowly.
Paul travaille plus lentement que Pierre.
Paul works more slowly than Pierre.

VOCABULARY 2

le banquier/la banquière	banker
le facteur/la factrice	postman/woman
le russe	Russian (language)
l'acteur/l'actrice	actor/actress
courageux	brave
distinct	distinct
beau (m.)	beautiful
bel (m. before a vowel or h)	
beaux (m. pl.)	
belle (f.)	
belles (f. pl.)	

Exercise 2

Translate:

1. The banker is richer than the teacher.
2. The postman is poorer than the lawyer (f.).
3. The pilot is as brave as the astronaut.
4. French is not as difficult as Russian.
   (say *the* French ... *the* Russian)
5. She speaks more distinctly than Paul.
6. He listens more attentively than his brother.

6

NOTE: We've seen that "than" is translated as **que**. However, when "than" is followed by a number, **de** is used in place of **que**:

J'ai plus de 40 euros. I have more than 40 euros.

6.5 SUPERLATIVE OF ADJECTIVES

In English, the superlative is formed by adding "-est" to the adjective or by using "most." In French, it is formed with **le plus**, **la plus**, or **les plus**:

Pierre est le plus petit de la classe.
Pierre is the smallest in the class.
Annette est la plus grande de la famille.
Annette is the tallest in the family.
Pierre et Nicole sont les plus intelligents du groupe.
Pierre and Nicole are the most intelligent in the group.
Michel est le plus jeune pilote de la compagnie aérienne.
Michel is the youngest pilot in the airline company.

Note that "in" is translated as **de** after a superlative.

If the adjective is one that normally follows the noun, **le/la/les** are placed both before and after the noun:

le vin le plus cher
the most expensive wine
les livres les plus intéressants
the most interesting books

6.6 SUPERLATIVE OF ADVERBS

With adverbs, the masculine form **le plus** is used, even if the person or thing carrying out the action is feminine:

Annette travaille le plus rapidement de tous.
Annette works the fastest of all.

6.7 BETTER, BEST, WORSE, WORST

There are a few irregular comparisons and superlatives:

bon (good)   **meilleur** (better) **le meilleur** (the best)
bonne   **meilleure**   **la meilleure** (f.)

mauvais (bad) **pire** (worse)   **le pire** (the worst)

Unlike in English, **plus mauvais** and **le plus mauvais** are also possible and, in fact, are more usual.

bien (well)   **mieux** (better) **le mieux** (the best)
peu (little)   **moins** (less)   **le moins** (the least)
beaucoup   **plus** (more)   **le plus** (the most)
  (much)

Examples:

Un bon restaurant	A good restaurant
Un meilleur restaurant	A better restaurant
Le meilleur restaurant	The best restaurant
Je chante bien.	I sing well.
Vous chantez mieux.	You sing better.
Il chante le mieux de tous.	He sings the best of all.

VOCABULARY 3

le parc	park
le monde	world
la ville	town, city
chic	elegant, stylish
célèbre	famous
agréable	pleasant
confortable	comfortable
impressionnant	impressive

6

Exercise 3

Respond to each sentence with the superlative:

Ce parc est grand. This park is large.
Oui, c'est le plus grand parc du monde.
Yes, this is the largest park in the world.

1. Ce restaurant est chic.
2. Cette librairie est grande.
3. Ce magasin est célèbre.
4. Cette cathédrale est belle.
5. Cette bière est bonne.
6. Ce parc est agréable.
7. Londres est une ville intéressante.
8. Cette voiture est confortable.
9. Cet avion est impressionnant.

6

6.8 TALKING ABOUT THE WEATHER

Like anyone, the French often discuss the weather. The verb **faire** or the expression **il y a** appears in many statements connected with this topic:

Il fait beau.	The weather is fine.
Il fait mauvais.	The weather is bad.
Il fait chaud.	It's hot.
Il fait froid.	It's cold.
Il y a du vent.	It's windy.
Il y a du soleil.	It's sunny.
Il y a du brouillard.	It's foggy.
Il pleut.	It's raining.
Il neige.	It's snowing.

Exercise 4

Which French expression describes the weather in the following situations?

1. An umbrella would be useful.
2. Due to poor visibility, there is a risk of road accidents.
3. Hold on to your hat!
4. You'll need a warm overcoat.
5. Dark glasses would be a great help.
6. It's nice when this happens at Christmas.
7. Open the window and let in a little cool air.
8. It's probably best to stay at home.
9. A walk through the park would be pleasant.

6.9 VERBS FORMING THE PAST WITH ÊTRE

6

We saw in section 4.1 that the present perfect tense of most French verbs is formed with **avoir** (to have):

j'ai téléphoné	I telephoned
vous avez fini	you finished

But some verbs, often denoting motion, form their past with **être**. The following verbs, some of which are irregular, are the most important:

aller (irreg.)	to go
arriver	to arrive
retourner	to return
monter	to go up
rester	to stay
partir (irreg.)	to leave
sortir (irreg.)	to go out
venir (irreg.)	to come
revenir (irreg.)	to come back
descendre	to go down

Examples:

je suis allé	I went
je suis arrivé	I arrived
il est parti	he left
il est sorti	he went out
vous êtes venu	you came
vous êtes descendu	you went down

NOTE: When **monter** and **descendre** mean, respectively, "to take up" and "to bring down," they form the perfect tenses with **avoir**.

With **être**, the past participles (**allé**, **parti**, **venu**, etc.) of these verbs must agree in gender and number with the person carrying out the action (the subject of the verb), just as if they were adjectives:

masculine singular	feminine singular
je suis allé	**je suis partie**
il est arrivé	**elle est sortie**
vous êtes retourné	**vous êtes venue**
tu es resté	**tu es descendue**

masculine plural	feminine plural
nous sommes allés	**nous sommes restées**
vous êtes partis	**vous êtes sorties**
ils sont revenus	**elles sont descendues**

VOCABULARY 4

le bureau	office	**tout** (m.)	all
la réunion	meeting	**tous** (m. pl.)	
la journée	day (daytime)	**toute** (f.)	
la maison	house, home	**toutes** (f. pl.)	
l'infirmier/ l'infirmière	nurse		
le/la docteur(e)	doctor		
l'étudiant(e)	student (university)		
l'élève (m./f.)	student, pupil, learner		

Exercise 5

A. Imagine for a moment the following:

You are a doctor (male). You arrived at the hospital this morning at 7 o'clock. You went to a meeting at 10 o'clock. You left the hospital with 2 nurses.

Now complete these sentences:

1. Je suis (doctor).
2. Ce matin je (arriver) à l'hôpital à 7 heures.
3. Je (aller) à une réunion à 10 heures.
4. Je (partir) avec 2 infirmières.

B. Imagine the following:

You are a journalist (female). Yesterday, you went to a press conference. At 1 o'clock, you went upstairs to the restaurant. You returned to the office very late.

Now complete these sentences:

1. Je suis (journalist).
2. Hier je (aller) à une conférence de presse.
3. Je (monter) au restaurant à 1 heure.
4. Je (retourner) au bureau très tard.

C. Consider the following:

Nicole and Sophie are students. They went to the university this morning at 9 o'clock. They stayed the whole day in the library. They came back home at 5 o'clock.

Now complete these sentences:

1. Nicole et Sophie sont (students).
2. Ce matin elles (aller) à l'université à 9 heures.
3. Elles (rester) toute la journée à la bibliothèque.
4. Elles (revenir) à la maison à 5 heures.

Exercise 6

Translate:

1. The engineers arrived yesterday.
2. The nurses (m.) have already left.
3. We (f.) came back early.
4. You (fam. sing. m.) went downstairs.
5. Did the doctor (f.) stay all day?
6. Did you come back very late?

6.10 THE USEFUL EXPRESSION **JE VOUDRAIS**

You'll often need to ask for things and to say what you would like to do. Use **je voudrais** (I would like):

Je voudrais un café.
I'd like a coffee.
Je voudrais de la confiture.
I'd like some jam.
Je voudrais prendre le petit déjeuner dans ma chambre.
I would like to have (lit. "take") breakfast in my room.
Je voudrais rester deux jours.
I would like to stay two days.

NOTE:

1. If you ask for **un café**, you will get an espresso. If you want a larger coffee with milk, ask for **un café crème** or, at breakfast time, **un café au lait**.

2. voudrais is actually the first-person singular of the conditional, which we will come to later!

VOCABULARY 6

le timbre	stamp
le plan	street map
le lait	milk
le sucre	sugar
le thé	tea
la carte postale	postcard
la note	bill (in a hotel)
l'addition (f.)	bill (in a restaurant)
régler	to settle, to pay

IRREGULAR VERB

envoyer (to send)

Present tense
j'envoie
tu envoies
il/elle envoie
nous envoyons
vous envoyez
ils/elles envoient

Exercise 7

Ask for the following using je voudrais:

1. a postcard
2. a stamp
3. a street map of the town
4. an American newspaper
5. some milk
6. some sugar
7. some tea

And now, say that you would like:

8. to telephone New York
9. to settle the hotel bill

6 6.11 USING THE EXPRESSION **IL FAUT** ("IT IS NECESSARY TO")

To say that something has to be done, you can use
il faut (I/you/we etc. must, it is necessary):

Il faut conduire à droite.
You have to drive on the right.
Il faut aller à la pharmacie.
You have to go to the pharmacy.

Also note this useful way of talking about what you need:

Il nous faut un dictionnaire.
We need a dictionary.
(lit. "It to us is necessary a dictionary.")

VOCABULARY 7

le crayon	pencil
le stylo	pen
le papier	paper
la gomme	eraser
l'enveloppe (f.)	envelope
l'allumette (f.)	match

Exercise 8

Say you need the following:

1. a pencil
2. a pen

Now she needs:

3. an eraser
4. some paper

Now they need:

5. some envelopes
6. some stamps
7. some matches

VOCABULARY 8

le port	port
le pain	bread
l'article (m.)	item
la place	square
la rue	street
la marque	brand
la promotion	special offer
la porte	door
l'année (f.)	year
tourner	to turn
recommander	to recommend
tout droit	straight ahead
à gauche	on/to the left
à droite	on/to the right
d'habitude	usually
au revoir	goodbye
si	so
voilà	there it is (pointing)
autre	other
rouge	red
quelques	a few
dernier,	last
dernière	

Un touriste passe la journée à Boulogne-sur-Mer

TOURISTE **Pardon, madame. Je cherche une bonne épicerie, ici près du port.**

PASSANTE **La meilleure épicerie de Boulogne est sur la place, en face de la banque. Vous allez tout droit et vous prenez la première rue à gauche.**

TOURISTE **Merci, madame. [Il répète] ... je vais tout droit, je tourne à droite ... non, non ... je tourne à gauche. Ah, voilà l'épicerie.**

EPICIÈRE **Bonjour, monsieur. Vous désirez?**

TOURISTE **Bonjour, madame. Je voudrais du fromage, du vin et de la bière, s'il vous plaît.**

EPICIÈRE **Voici le fromage. C'est la meilleure marque. Il est plus cher que les autres fromages, mais il est excellent. Je vous recommande aussi ce vin rouge. Il est moins cher que d'habitude; il est en promotion.**

TOURISTE **Bien. Je prends ces trois articles. Merci. Est-ce que vous vendez aussi du pain?**

EPICIÈRE **Non, monsieur. Pour cela, il faut aller à la boulangerie. La boulangerie est à côté du bureau de poste.**

TOURISTE **Merci. Au revoir, madame. [Il va à la porte] ... Oh, il pleut! Et il y a du vent.**

EPICIÈRE **Attendez quelques instants. Ici à Boulogne il fait rarement beau. Il pleut souvent et il y a toujours du vent.**

TOURISTE **Oui. L'année dernière, ma femme et moi, nous sommes venus passer la journée ici, mais il a fait si mauvais. Nous avons attendu un jour, deux jours. Finalement, nous sommes restés une semaine à Boulogne!**

6

A tourist spends the day in Boulogne-sur-Mer

TOURIST Excuse me. I'm looking for a good little food shop, here near the port.

PASSERBY The best deli in Boulogne is in (on) the square, across from the bank. You go straight ahead and you take the first street on the left.

TOURIST Thank you. [He repeats] ... I go straight ahead, I turn right ... no, no ... I turn left. Ah, there's the deli.

SHOPKEEPER Good morning, sir. What would you like? [Literally "you wish?"]

TOURIST Good morning. I'd like some cheese, some wine, and some beer, please.

SHOPKEEPER Here's the cheese. It's the best brand. It's more expensive than the other cheeses, but it's excellent. I also recommend this red wine. It's less expensive than usual; it's a special offer.

TOURIST Fine. I'll take [lit. "I take"] these three items. Thank you. Do you sell bread?

SHOPKEEPER No, sir. For that you have to go to the bakery. The bakery is next to the post office.

TOURIST Thank you. [He goes to the door]... Oh, it's raining. And it's windy.

SHOPKEEPER Wait a few moments. Here in Boulogne, the weather's rarely fine. It often rains and it's always windy.

TOURIST Yes. Last year my wife and I came to spend the day here, but the weather was so bad. We waited ... We waited one day, two days. In the end, we stayed in Boulogne for a week!

Week 7

- Adverbs of quantity ("much", "many", "enough", etc.)
- The future tense (including the irregular forms of some key verbs)
- The all-important modal verbs **pouvoir**, **devoir**, **vouloir**, and **savoir**
- Countries
- More numbers (up to 100)
- Four more irregular verbs

7.1 QUANTITY: MUCH, MANY, ENOUGH, ETC.

On occasion, you will need to talk about quantities— you may have too much of something, or too little, or not enough, and so on.

Here are some useful words for talking about quantity:

beaucoup	much, many, a lot of
trop	too much, too many
tant	so much, so many
peu	little, few
assez	enough

When a noun follows these words, they are linked by **de (d')**:

beaucoup de temps (m.)	much/a lot of time
beaucoup de légumes (m.)	many vegetables
trop d'argent	too much money
trop de vêtements (m.)	too many clothes
peu de patience (f.)	little patience
assez de fruits (m. pl.)	enough fruit

The following are also linked to the noun by **de (d')**:

plus	more
moins	less, fewer
autant	as much, as many

Examples:

J'ai l'intention de boire plus d'eau.
I intend to drink more water.
J'ai l'intention de manger moins de pain.
I intend to eat less bread.
Alex a autant d'argent que Cécile.
Alex has as much money as Cécile.

VOCABULARY 1

le chapeau	hat
le pantalon	pants
le foulard	scarf
le gilet	cardigan (also vest)
le costume	suit
la chemise	shirt
la cravate	tie
la robe	dress
la jupe	skirt

7

Exercise 1

Answer the questions.

Example:
Vous faut-il une chemise? Do you need a shirt?
Non, j'ai beaucoup de chemises. No, I have a lot of shirts.

1. Vous faut-il une cravate?
2. Vous faut-il un costume?
3. Vous faut-il une robe?

Example:
Michel a acheté un chapeau? Has Michel bought a hat?
Oui, il a maintenant trop de chapeaux. Yes, he now has too many hats.

4. Bernard a acheté un pantalon?
5. Hélène a acheté une jupe?
6. Marie a acheté un foulard?

Translate:

7. He has little patience.
8. Have you put enough shirts in the suitcase?
9. I have more cardigans than Manon.
10. You have fewer suits than Pierre.

7

You may need to talk about what you plan to do in the future. There are three ways of doing this:

1. In conversation, you can often use the present tense with a future meaning:

Un petit instant, je finis ce rapport.
One moment, I'll just finish this report.
Bien. Je prends ces trois articles.
Fine. I'll take these three items.
J'arrive lundi.
I'll arrive on Monday.

2. As in English, you can use "to go" (conjugated) followed by another verb (in the infinitive):

Je vais téléphoner demain.
I'm going to call tomorrow.
Aujourd'hui il va manger dans un restaurant chic.
Today he's going to eat in a classy restaurant.
Nous allons regarder la télévision ce soir.
We're going to watch television this evening.

3. You can use the future tense, which is formed by adding the following endings to the infinitive of the verb:

je	**- ai**
tu	**- as**
il/elle	**- a**
nous	**- ons**
vous	**- ez**
ils/elles	**- ont**

Examples:
je consulterai	I will consult
tu chanteras	you (fam.) will sing
il mangera	he will eat

elle exportera	she will export
nous choisirons	we will choose
vous finirez	you will finish
ils garantiront	they will guarantee
elles réussiront	they (f.) will succeed

To form the future of **-re** verbs, drop the final **e** of the infinitive before adding the endings:

j'attendrai	I will wait
tu descendras	you will go down
il apprendra	he will learn
nous comprendrons	we will understand
vous mettrez	you will put
ils promettront	they will promise

Some common verbs are irregular in the future tense, so you'll need to learn them:

avoir	**j'aurai**	I will have
être	**je serai**	I will be
aller	**j'irai**	I will go
faire	**je ferai**	I will do, make
venir	**je viendrai**	I will come
envoyer	**j'enverrai**	I will send
il y a	**il y aura**	there will be
il faut	**il faudra**	it will be necessary

7

VOCABULARY 2

le tennis	tennis
le week-end	weekend
le père/la mère	father/mother
l'appartement (m.)	apartment
la réunion	meeting
la conférence	conference
les courses (f.)	shopping
international	international
étudier	to study
réparer	to repair
jouer	to play
visiter	to visit
ranger	to tidy, to put away
organiser	to organize

IRREGULAR VERB

écrire (to write)

Present tense
j'écris
tu écris
il/elle écrit
nous écrivons
vous écrivez
ils/elles écrivent

Present perfect
j'ai écrit, etc.

7

Exercise 2

Here is a list of things you plan to do tomorrow (**demain**). Translate the list into French, using the construction with **aller**. Write complete sentences.

1. Listen to the radio
2. Buy a newspaper
3. Study French
4. Do the shopping

Here is Djibril's list for next week (**la semaine prochaine**). Translate using the future tense in complete sentences:

5. Repair the car
6. Play tennis
7. Write a letter
8. Visit the museum

Here is Paul and Camille's list for next month (**le mois prochain**). Use the future tense and write complete sentences:

9. Tidy the apartment
10. Organize a meeting
11. Go to an international conference
12. Spend a weekend in London

Translate:

13. She will finish her letter.
14. We will go to the theater next week.
15. You will surprise your father.
16. You (fam.) will choose your dress next month.

Modal verbs are auxiliary verbs that are used to express an idea (such as possibility, ability, or necessity) about the main verb—e.g. "I can come" or "We must call." There are four important modal verbs in French:

pouvoir to be able to (can)
devoir to have to (must)
vouloir to want to
savoir to know (how to)

1. Pouvoir
To talk about what you can or cannot do, use the irregular verb **pouvoir**:

Present tense
je peux, I can, I am able to
tu peux
il/elle peut
nous pouvons
vous pouvez
ils/elles peuvent

Past tense (present perfect)
j'ai pu, I was able to

Future tense
je pourrai, I will be able to

Modal verb (conjugated) + main verb (infinitive):
Je peux faire les courses maintenant.
I can do the shopping now.
Pouvez-vous me dire où est la gare?
Can you tell me where the station is?
Avez-vous pu téléphoner à Paris ?
Have you been able to call Paris?

You might hear **puis-je** in place of **est-ce que je peux** to express "may I …?", but this is very formal, so it is mainly used with a hint of irony today.

2. Devoir

To talk about what you must or have to do, use the
irregular verb **devoir** (this can also mean "should"):

Present tense
je dois, I have to, I must, I should
tu dois
il/elle doit
nous devons
vous devez
ils/elles doivent

Past tense (present perfect)
j'ai dû, I had to, I should have

Future tense
je devrai, I will have to

Examples:
Je dois changer de vie.
I have to change my life.
Vous devez envoyer une carte postale à votre ami.
You should send a postcard to your friend.
Il a dû partir.
He had to leave.
Elle devra apprendre l'espagnol.
She will have to learn Spanish.

3. Vouloir

You've already seen **je voudrais**, meaning "I would like."
It comes from the irregular verb **vouloir** (to want):

Present tense:
je veux, I want
tu veux
il/elle veut
nous voulons
vous voulez
ils/elles veulent

Past tense (present perfect)
j'ai voulu, I wanted

Future tense
je voudrai, I will want

Examples:
Je veux changer mon argent américain en euros.
I want to change my American money into euros.
Nous voulons une chambre pour deux personnes.
We want a double room.

A request can be made more polite by putting
Voulez-vous ... at the beginning of the sentence:
Voulez-vous signer ici? Will you sign here?

4. Savoir
This irregular verb means "to know":

Present tense
je sais, I know
tu sais
il/elle sait
nous savons
vous savez
ils/elles savent

Past tense (present perfect)
j'ai su, I knew

Future tense
je saurai, I will know

Examples:
Je sais que vous voyagez à l'étranger.
I know that you travel abroad.
Savez-vous où je peux louer une voiture?
Do you know where I can hire/rent a car?
Lucas saura demain s'il va être au chômage.
Lucas will know tomorrow if he's going to be
unemployed. (lit. "at-the unemployment")

Savoir can also mean "to know how to":

Je sais jouer du piano.
I can (know how to) play the piano.

Note the difference between **pouvoir** and **savoir**:

Je ne sais pas jouer du piano.
I can't play the piano. (I don't know how)
Je ne peux pas jouer du piano.
I can't play the piano. (my hand is bandaged)

VOCABULARY 3

le/la diplomate	diplomat
le marché	market
le contrat	contract
l'écriture (f.)	handwriting
arrêter	to stop
arrêter de fumer	to stop smoking
décourager	to discourage
nager	to swim
garer	to park
faire le tour du monde	to travel around the world

IRREGULAR VERB

conduire (to drive)

Present tense
je conduis
tu conduis
il/elle conduit
nous conduisons
vous conduisez
ils/elles conduisent

Present perfect
j'ai conduit, etc.

Exercise 3

Say that you can:

1. buy the vegetables at the market
2. prepare the report

Say that we cannot:

3. arrive on Monday
4. read his handwriting

Say that she must:

5. sign the contract
6. stop smoking

Say that they must not:

7. discourage the students
8. park the car in front of the hospital

Say that he wants to:

9. travel around the world
10. spend less money

Ask your friend whether he/she knows how to:

11. drive
12. swim

In French, some countries are masculine and some are feminine. Here are some examples:

le Danemark	Denmark
le Portugal	Portugal
le Luxembourg	Luxemburg
le Canada	Canada
le Japon	Japan
le Pays de Galles	Wales
les États-Unis (m.)	United States
le Royaume-Uni	United Kingdom
la France	France
la Belgique	Belgium
la Grande-Bretagne	Great Britain
la Grèce	Greece
les Pays-Bas	Netherlands
la Chine	China
la Russie	Russia
l'Angleterre (f.)	England
l'Ecosse (f.)	Scotland
l'Allemagne (f.)	Germany
l'Italie (f.)	Italy
l'Espagne (f.)	Spain
l'Irlande (f.)	Ireland

Before a masculine country, "in" or "to" is translated **au**:

au Pays de Galles	in/to Wales
au Portugal	in/to Portugal
au Japon	in/to Japan

Before a feminine country, "in" or "to" is translated **en**:

en Angleterre	in/to England
en Écosse	in/to Scotland
en France	in/to France
en Chine	in/to China

For a country that is plural, **aux** is used:

aux États-Unis	in/to the United States

Exercise 4

With your book closed, write a list of 15 countries, indicating whether they are masculine or feminine. Then check your list.

Exercise 5

Translate:

1. We spend our vacations in Greece.
2. Do you (fam.) intend to go to Japan?
3. Germany exports cars to France.
4. Has the diplomat arrived in Russia?

7.5 NUMBERS

Let's continue with the numbers in French:

63 **soixante-trois**	81 **quatre-vingt-un**
70 **soixante-dix**	82 **quatre-vingt-deux**
71 **soixante et onze**	88 **quatre-vingt-huit**
72 **soixante-douze**	90 **quatre-vingt-dix**
73 **soixante-treize**	91 **quatre-vingt-onze**
79 **soixante-dix-neuf**	99 **quatre-vingt-dix-neuf**
80 **quatre-vingts**	100 **cent**

Note that the **s** in **quatre-vingts** is omitted when another number follows.

Exercise 6

Complete the following, writing the answers in words:

a. 10 + 10 =	**g.** 40 + 30 =
b. 10 + 12 =	**h.** 19 + 60 =
c. 11 + 20 =	**i.** 40 + 41 =
d. 27 + 20 =	**j.** 41 + 50 =
e. 30 + 29 =	**k.** 19 + 80 =
f. 21 + 40 =	**l.** 50 + 50 =

VOCABULARY 4

la résolution	resolution
la liste	list
la promesse	promise
avoir l'intention (de)	to intend (to), to plan (to)
la santé	health
certain / certaine (m. / f.)	certain
neuf / neuve (m. / f.)	new
quoi	what
Quoi de neuf?	What's new? What's up?
eh bien ...	well ...
vraiment	really
ça = cela	that
souhaiter	to wish, to want
décider (de)	to decide (to)
excuser	to excuse

IRREGULAR VERBS

boire (to drink)   **dire** (to say, to tell)

Present tense	Present tense
je bois	**je dis**
tu bois	**tu dis**
il/elle boit	**il/elle dit**
nous buvons	**nous disons**
vous buvez	**vous dites**
ils/elles boivent	**ils/elles disent**

Present perfect	Present perfect
j'ai bu, etc.	**j'ai dit**, etc.

7

CONVERSATION

Hélène prend des résolutions pour la nouvelle année

KARIM Bonjour, Hélène. Je suis venu vous souhaiter une bonne année.

HÉLÈNE Bonjour, Karim. Bonne année à vous aussi.

KARIM Quoi de neuf?

HÉLÈNE Eh bien, j'ai décidé de changer de vie. J'ai pris beaucoup de résolutions pour la nouvelle année.

KARIM Vraiment? Et quelles sont ces résolutions?

HÉLÈNE Voici ma liste:
1. Je vais maigrir.
2. Je vais regarder la télévision moins souvent.
3. Je mangerai plus de légumes.
4. Je mangerai plus de fruits.
5. Je dépenserai moins d'argent en vêtements.
Mon mari m'a fait aussi quelques promesses. Voici sa liste:
1. Il va boire moins de bière.
2. Il va boire plus d'eau.
3. Il arrêtera de fumer.
4. Il fera du sport chaque matin.
5. Il rentrera plus tôt à la maison le soir.

KARIM Et vous pensez que vous serez plus heureux?

HÉLÈNE Oui. Nous aurons plus de temps et plus d'argent. Nous serons tous les deux en meilleure santé.

KARIM Et comment est-ce que vous dépenserez tout cet argent?

HÉLÈNE Nous achèterons une voiture électrique. Nous voyagerons à l'étranger. Nous irons au Japon. Nous irons en Chine et aux États-Unis. Nous ferons le tour du monde.

KARIM Excusez-moi, mais je dois dire que j'ai déjà entendu ça. Je l'ai entendu l'année dernière. Je ne veux pas vous décourager, mais je suis certain que vous ne ferez jamais rien!

Hélène makes ["takes"] some New Year resolutions

KARIM Good morning, Hélène. I've come to wish you a Happy New Year.

HÉLÈNE Good morning, Karim. Happy New Year to you, too.

KARIM What's new?

HÉLÈNE Well, I've decided to change my life. I've made a lot of resolutions for the new year.

KARIM Really? And what are these resolutions?

HÉLÈNE Here's my list:
1. I'm going to lose weight.
2. I'm going to watch television less often.
3. I'll eat more vegetables.
4. I'll eat more fruit.
5. I'll spend less money on [literally "in"] clothes.
My husband has also made me a few promises.
Here's his list:
1. He's going to drink less beer.
2. He's going to drink more water.
3. He'll stop smoking.
4. He'll exercise each morning.
5. He'll come home earlier in the evening.

KARIM Do you think you'll be happier?

HÉLÈNE Yes. We'll have more time and more money.
We'll both [literally "all the two"] be in better health.

KARIM And how will you spend all this money?

HÉLÈNE We'll buy an electric car. We'll travel abroad. We'll go to Japan. We'll go to China and to the United States. We'll travel around the world [literally "We'll do the tour of the world"].

KARIM I'm sorry [literally "Excuse me"], but I have to say that I've heard all that before [literally "I've already heard that"]. I heard it last year. I don't want to discourage you, but I'm sure that you'll never do anything! [literally "that you will never do nothing"].

Week 8

- The imperfect tense ("used to do," "was doing")
- Relative pronouns ("who," "whom," "which," "that")
- The conditional ("would")
- More about pronouns
- The distinction between **savoir** and **connaître** both meaning "to know"

8.1 THE IMPERFECT TENSE ("USED TO DO," "WAS DOING")

We've already seen how the present perfect tense is used to talk about the past:

J'ai acheté un livre.

This tense is used to describe a completed action in the past: "I have bought a book" or "I bought a book."

But a different tense is used to say what you used to do at some period in your life: the imperfect tense. To form this tense, take the **nous** form of the present tense, drop the **-ons** ending, and add:

je	- ais	nous	- ions
tu	- ais	vous	- iez
il/elle	- ait	ils/elles	- aient

There is only one exception to the above rule, and that's the verb **être**.

Examples:

je fumais	I used to smoke
tu chantais	you (fam.) used to sing
il organisait	he used to organize
elle choisissait	she used to choose
nous finissions	we used to finish
vous vendiez	you used to sell
ils lisaient	they used to read
elles écrivaient	they used to write

j'étais I used to be (I was)
il était he used to be (he was)
etc.

j'avais I used to have (I had)
il avait he used to have (he had)
etc.

The imperfect tense is also used when translating such sentences as "I was reading the newspaper when the telephone rang." In other words, if the English construction is "was/were ...-ing," the imperfect tense is required in French.

Examples:
J'écoutais la radio, quand Michel a téléphoné.
I was listening to the radio when Michel telephoned.
Il prenait une douche, quand le facteur est arrivé.
He was taking a shower when the postman arrived.

VOCABULARY 1

le bruit	noise
le porte-monnaie	coin purse, wallet
le cambrioleur	burglar
la traduction	translation
en haut	upstairs
en bas	downstairs
collectionner	to collect
jouer au football	to play soccer (football)
aller à la pêche	to go fishing
faire de la photo(graphie)	to do photography
entrer dans la maison	to enter the house

8

Exercise 1

Here are some things that Bernard and Chantal used to do when they were younger. Translate them using the imperfect tense:

1. He used to play soccer (football).
2. He used to go fishing.
3. He used to collect stamps.
4. She used to sing.
5. She used to listen to records.

Now translate:

6. We used to learn Spanish.
7. We used to live in a small house.
8. We used to do photography.
9. I was finishing the translation when I heard a noise upstairs.
10. She was doing the shopping when she lost her wallet.
11. They were watching television when the burglar entered the house.

8

8.2 RELATIVE PRONOUNS: WHO, WHOM, WHICH, THAT

The main relative pronouns in French are:

qui   who, which, that (subject)
que   whom, which, that (object)

Note: **que** becomes **qu'** in front of a vowel or h.

Examples:
L'automobiliste qui parle français.
The motorist who speaks French.
La voiture qui est en panne.
The car that has broken down.
(lit. "that is in breakdown")

L'auto-stoppeur que j'ai pris.
The hitchhiker whom I picked up.
Le camion que vous avez réparé.
The truck that you repaired.

If you're having difficulty deciding if "who," "which," "that" is the subject or the object, here's a rule to help you:

• If in English the verb comes immediately after "who," "which," "that," use **qui**
• If in English there is another word between "who," "which," "that" and the verb, use **que**

Examples:
the car that has broken down	**qui**
the car that I prefer	**que**

NOTE: In English, "whom," "which," and "that" are sometimes omitted, but they must always be expressed in French:

Le moteur que vous vérifiez.
The engine (that) you are checking.

We learned in section 5.7 that in the perfect tenses, the verb (**invité, trouvé**) has to reflect the gender and number of the object pronoun such as "me" or "him" used with it; the same principle applies to **que**:

Voici le permis de conduire que j'ai trouvé.
Here is the driver's license that I found.
Voici la carte que j'ai achetée.
Here's the map that I bought.
Voici les pneus que j'ai choisis.
Here are the tires that I've chosen.

After a preposition, "whom" is also translated by **qui**:

Où est le mécanicien à qui vous avez téléphoné?
Where's the mechanic you called?
(lit. "Where's the mechanic to whom you telephoned?")

8

BUT "which" after a preposition is translated as follows:

lequel (m.)   **lesquels** (m. pl.)
laquelle (f.)   **lesquelles** (f. pl.)

The above words combine with **à** and **de** in the usual way: **auquel, duquel, desquels, desquelles**.

For example:
Le cric avec lequel il a changé la roue.
The jack with which he changed the wheel.
La galerie sur laquelle nous avons mis les valises.
The roof rack on which we put the suitcases.
Le garage auquel elle a envoyé son chèque.
The garage to which she sent her check.

In place of **de qui, duquel, de laquelle, desquels, desquelles**, the word **dont** (of which) is often used:

L'autoroute dont nous parlons.
The highway that we're speaking about.
(lit. "The highway of which we speak.")

The term **dont** is also used to mean "whose":

L'automobiliste dont la voiture est électrique.
The driver whose car is electric.
Le garagiste dont je connais le frère.
The garage owner whose brother I know.

Note the unexpected word order in the last French sentence.

Also note the use of **ce qui** (subject) or **ce que** (object) where in English we would use "what" as a linking word:

Je ne peux pas lire ce qui est écrit ici.
I cannot read what is written here.
Je ne peux pas lire ce que Michel a écrit ici.
I cannot read what Michel has written here.

8

VOCABULARY 2

le petit déjeuner	breakfast
la télévision/	television
le téléviseur	
le/la réceptionniste	receptionist
le fils/la fille	son, daughter (or girl)
l'ascenseur (m.)	elevator (lift)
l'homme/femme	cleaner
de ménage	
lourd	heavy
bilingue	bilingual
malade	ill
correct	correct
apporter	to bring
commander	to order
marcher	to walk, to work (machines)
donner sur	to overlook

Exercise 2

Translate:

1. The hotel that you are looking for is on the right.
2. I would like the room that overlooks the park.
3. The room, which we have reserved for you, is next to the elevator.
4. I've brought the breakfast that your husband ordered.
5. Where's the television that doesn't work?
6. The suitcases, which are in the hall, are very heavy.
7. The receptionist (f.) to whom you spoke is bilingual.
8. The client (m.), whose son is ill, is in room 5.
9. Didn't you understand what the cleaner (f.) said to you?
10. The bill that you have prepared is correct.

THE CONDITIONAL ("WOULD" AND THE CONSTRUCTION "IF I HAD ... I WOULD ...")

The conditional ("would") is formed by adding the following endings to the infinitive of the verb:

je	-ais	nous	-ions
tu	-ais	vous	-iez
il/elle	-ait	ils/elles	-aient

As with the future tense, if the infinitive ends in **-re**, omit the final **e** before adding the endings.

Examples:

je louerais	I would hire/rent
tu inviterais	you (fam.) would invite
il habiterait	he would live
elle étudierait	she would study
nous choisirions	we would choose
vous finiriez	you would finish
ils comprendraient	they would understand
elles écriraient	they would write

When a verb is irregular in the future tense, it has the same irregularity in the conditional:

j'aurais	I would have
tu serais	you (fam.) would be
il irait	he would go
elle ferait	she would do/make
nous enverrions	we would send
vous pourriez	you could, would be able to
ils voudraient	they would like
elles sauraient	they would know
il faudrait	it would be necessary
il y aurait	there would be

The "if" part of a conditional sentence (i.e. "if I had the time," "if I spoke French," etc.) is expressed by **si** (if) and the imperfect.

si j'avais le temps if I had the time
s'il parlait français if he spoke French
si vous vendiez votre maison if you sold your house

Note: **si** becomes **s'** before **il** and **ils**.

The conditional is also used in French when the speaker or writer is repeating something he or she has heard but is unable to vouch for its accuracy. Compare:

Le client a donné son consentement au contrat.
The client has given his consent to the contract.
Le client aurait donné son consentement au contrat.
Apparently, the client has (lit. "would have") given his consent to the contract.

VOCABULARY 3

le travail	work
l'interprète (m. and f.)	interpreter
l'enfant (m. and f.)	child
le portugais	Portuguese (language)
marié(e)	married
comme	as
dessiner	to draw

IRREGULAR VERB

peindre (to paint)

Present tense
je peins
tu peins
il/elle peint
nous peignons
vous peignez
ils/elles peignent

Present perfect
j'ai peint, etc.

8

Exercise 3

Answer the questions as follows:

Qu'est-ce que vous feriez, si vous aviez beaucoup de temps?
What would you do, if you had a lot of time?
(write a book)

Si j'avais beaucoup de temps, j'écrirais un livre.
If I had a lot of time, I would write a book.

1. Qu'est-ce que vous feriez, si vous étiez riche? (travel around the world)

2. Qu'est-ce que vous feriez, si vous ne travailliez pas? (paint and draw)

3. Qu'est-ce que Pierre ferait, s'il avait beaucoup de temps? (learn Portuguese)

4. Qu'est-ce que Nicole ferait, si elle parlait français? (work as an interpreter)

5. Qu'est-ce que Samira ferait, si elle parlait allemand? (work as a bilingual teacher)

6. Qu'est-ce que je ferais, si j'étais marié? (buy a house)

7. Qu'est-ce qu'ils feraient, s'ils étaient au chômage? (look for work)

8. Qu'est-ce qu'elles feraient, si elles avaient des enfants? (go to the park)

9. Qu'est-ce que tu ferais, si tu avais le temps? (read a great deal)

10. Qu'est-ce que nous ferions, si nous voulions maigrir? (eat less and exercise)

8

8.4 MORE ABOUT PRONOUNS

We've already seen in section 5.6 how "me," "him," "her,"
"to us," "to you," etc. are expressed in French when
these pronouns are the object of a verb. But some of
these pronouns have a different form when they:

1. follow a preposition
2. form part of a comparison
3. stand alone
4. follow the verb **être** (to be)

In these cases, use the following pronouns:

moi	I, me	**nous**	we, us
toi	you (fam.)	**vous**	you
lui	he, him	**eux**	they, them (m.)
elle	she, her	**elles**	they, them (f.)

Examples:
Est-ce qu'il y a des lettres pour moi?
Are there any letters for me?
Je travaille en face de lui.
I work across from him.
Nous sommes partis sans eux.
We left without them.
Il est plus petit que moi.
He's smaller than me.
Qui parle anglais ici? Elle.
Who speaks English here? She does.
C'est lui qui écrit toutes les lettres.
He's the one who (lit. "It's he who") writes all the letters.

8

Exercise 4

Replace the words in italics with a pronoun:

1. Je suis arrivé avec *Paul*.
2. Je voudrais avoir une place à côté de *la directrice*.
3. Nous avons l'intention de partir sans *Antoine et Julie*.
4. Anne est plus travailleuse que *les nouvelles infirmières*.
5. Michelle est moins paresseuse que *le nouveau programmeur*.
6. Qui a cassé mon poste de radio? *La femme de ménage.*
7. C'est *la présidente* et *le premier ministre* qui ont signé le traité hier.

8.5 SAVOIR AND CONNAÎTRE ("TO KNOW")

In section 7.3 we learned that "to know" is translated by **savoir**. This verb means to know a fact:

Savez-vous où est Paul?
Do you know where Paul is?
Je sais à quelle heure le train part.
I know what time the train leaves.

BUT, when talking about knowing a person or a place—
that is, when the meaning is "to be acquainted with"—
then you need to use the irregular verb **connaître**:

Present tense
je connais, I know, I am acquainted with
tu connais
il/elle connaît
nous connaissons
vous connaissez
ils/elles connaissent

Present perfect
j'ai connu, I knew, I was acquainted with

Examples:
Je connais Paul, mais je ne sais pas où il habite.
I know Paul, but I don't know where he lives.
Vous connaissez Paris?
Do you know Paris?

VOCABULARY 5

l'oncle	uncle
la tante	aunt
libre	free, available
occupé	occupied, busy

8

Exercise 5

Translate:

1. I don't know if Jules has finished his work.
2. I don't know the Duponts.
3. Do you know where I can hire a computer?
4. Do you know if the doctor is free?
5. Does Nabila know my aunt?

Exercise 6

In the conversation at the end of this chapter, change all the familiar forms (tu, te, toi, ton) into the more formal vous/votre forms and make all the necessary changes to the verbs.

VOCABULARY 6

le cas	case, situation
les gens (m. pl.)	people
la visite	visit
la porte	door
la retraite	retirement
au-dessus de	above
chez	at someone's home or shop
bonsoir	good evening
justement	just
si	so, yes (emphatic use after a negative)
à propos	by the way
à mi-temps	part time
tout de suite	immediately
trop	too
inattendu	unexpected
bruyant	noisy
déranger	to disturb
arranger	to suit
frapper	to knock
penser à	to think of (something)
penser de	to think of (opinion)
espérer	to hope

(See section 12.5 for how **espérer** slightly changes its spelling in the present tense.)

Une visite inattendue

PIERRE   **Bonsoir Nicole, j'espère que je ne te dérange pas.**

NICOLE   **Pierre! Bonsoir. Je pensais justement à toi.**

PIERRE   **Tu n'es pas trop occupée?**

NICOLE   **Non, non. J'écrivais une lettre, quand tu as frappé à la porte.**

PIERRE   **Ah bon? A qui est-ce que tu écrivais?**

NICOLE   **Aux Dupont.**

PIERRE   **Les Dupont? Je ne les connais pas.**

NICOLE   **Mais si! Les Dupont sont les gens qui habitaient au-dessus de chez nous à Paris, qui voyageaient beaucoup et dont les enfants étaient si bruyants.**

PIERRE   **Ah oui. Je ne les connaissais pas très bien. À propos, comment va ton travail?**

NICOLE   **Pas trop bien. Si seulement je pouvais travailler à mi-temps, ça m'arrangerait bien.**

PIERRE   **Qu'est-ce que tu ferais de tout ce temps libre?**

NICOLE   **Je peindrais, je dessinerais. Michel et moi, nous sortirions plus souvent, nous irions au cinéma, au restaurant. Je ferais du sport, j'apprendrais l'anglais, je lirais tous les livres que j'ai achetés l'année dernière, je …**

PIERRE   **Tu ferais mieux de prendre ta retraite tout de suite!**

8

An unexpected visit

PIERRE   Good evening, Nicole, I hope I'm not disturbing you.

NICOLE   Pierre! Good evening. I was just thinking of you.

PIERRE   You're not too busy?

NICOLE   No, no. I was writing a letter when you knocked at the door.

PIERRE   Really? [literally "oh good?"] Who were you writing to?

NICOLE   To the Duponts.

PIERRE   The Duponts? I don't know them.

NICOLE   Yes, you do! The Duponts are the people who used to live above us [literally "above at our place"] in Paris, who used to travel a lot, and whose children were so noisy.

PIERRE   Oh yes. I didn't know them very well. By the way, how's your work going?

NICOLE   Not too well. If only I could work part time that would suit me fine.

PIERRE   What would you do with [literally "of"] all that free time?

NICOLE   I'd paint, I'd draw. Michel and I [literally "Michel and I, we"] would go out more often, we'd go to the cinema, to restaurants. I'd exercise, I'd learn English, I'd read all the books I bought last year, I …

PIERRE   The best thing for you would be to retire immediately! [literally "You would do better to take your retirement immediately!"]

8

Self-assessment test 2 A–C

This self-assessment test, based on weeks 5–8, will enable you to check on your progress and see whether you need to review anything. Deduct one point for every grammatical mistake or wrong spelling. The answers and score assessment are in the key.

A. Prepositions   Total: 8 points
Complete the following:

1. Il y a un taxi [in front of] l'hôtel.
2. Il y a un restaurant [next to] la banque.
3. Il y a une librairie [across from] l'université.
4. Il y a un tunnel [under] la Manche.
5. Est-ce qu'il y a un hôtel [near] la gare?
6. C'est difficile de travailler [without] mon portable.
7. Nous pouvons manger [after] le spectacle.
8. Téléphonez [before] neuf heures.

B. The present perfect   Total: 10 points
Imagine that you are a journalist (male or female). This morning, you arrived at the hotel at seven o'clock. You went to an international conference at ten o'clock. You left very late. Now complete these sentences:

1. Je suis j....
2. Ce m... je ... ... à l'hôtel à sept heures.
3. Je ... ... à une c... i ... à dix heures.
4. Je ... ... très t....

C. The weather   Total: 10 points
Suggest the likely weather at the times and in the places indicated:

1. En Grande-Bretagne, au mois d'avril.
2. À Nice, au mois d'août.
3. À Londres, au mois de novembre.
4. En Russie, au mois de décembre.
5. En Écosse, en hiver.

8

D. Countries   Total: 12 points

Below are some simple clues to the names of countries. Identify the country and give its French name.

1. Son porto est très bon.
2. Le mont Fuji-Yama.
3. La statue de la Liberté.
4. La capitale? Athènes.
5. Cervantès.
6. Léonard de Vinci.
7. Ses tulipes sont belles.
8. La Révolution culturelle.
9. La capitale? Bruxelles.
10. Liberté, Egalité, Fraternité.
11. Shakespeare.
12. La capitale? Copenhague.

E. Numbers   Total: 14 points

Complete the following, writing the totals in words:

a. 30 + 28
b. 40 + 30
c. 15 + 60
d. 40 + 43
e. 50 + 40
f. 10 + 89
g. 50 + 50

F. The imperfect tense   Total: 14 points

Talk about your French friends, Emma and Léo:

1. He used to play soccer (football).
2. She used to learn English.
3. They used to live in a large house.
4. They were doing the shopping when she lost her wallet.

G. The conditional   Total: 8 points

"If only …." Answer the questions as indicated:

1. Qu'est-ce que vous feriez, si vous étiez riche?
[visit Japan and China]

2. Qu'est-ce que Maëlys ferait, si elle parlait italien?
[work as an interpreter]

3. Qu'est-ce que je ferais, si j'étais au chômage?
[look for work—use "tu"]

4. Qu'est-ce que nous ferions, si nous avions beaucoup de temps?
[read a great deal—use "nous"]

H. Do you remember …?   Total: 4 points

a. What's the difference between the verbs "savoir" and "connaître," both meaning "to know"?

b. What's the difference in meaning between "je ne sais pas jouer du piano" and "je ne peux pas jouer du piano"?

I. Conversation (role-play)   Total: 20 points

Play the part of Léa in this dialogue:

LÉA I've decided to change my life. I'm going to watch television less often. I'll eat more fruit. I'll exercise each morning. I'll spend less money on clothes.

KARIM Tu penses que tu seras plus heureuse?

LÉA Yes, I'll have more time and more money, and I'll be in better health.

8

Week 9

- *Demonstrative pronouns ("this one," "that one," "these," "those")*
- *Possessive pronouns ("mine," "yours," "hers," etc.)*
- *More about forming questions*
- *More about adverbs and adverbial expressions*
- *More irregular verbs*

9.1 DEMONSTRATIVE PRONOUNS: THIS ONE, THAT ONE, THESE, THOSE

In English, a sentence such as "I prefer my doctor to the doctor who came this morning" would normally be shortened to "I prefer my doctor to the one who came this morning." In French, "the one," "those," etc. are expressed as follows:

celui (m.)	the one
ceux (m. pl.)	those
celle (f.)	the one
celles (f. pl.)	those

Examples:
Je préfère mon médecin à celui qui est venu ce matin.
I prefer my doctor to the one who came this morning.
Cette infirmière et celle qui a pris votre tension.
This nurse and the one who took your blood pressure.
J'ai apporté vos comprimés et ceux de votre mari.
I've brought your tablets and your husband's (lit. "those of your husband").

In English, "this dentist and that dentist" would be "this dentist and that one." In French, "this one," "that one," "these," and "those" become:

masculine		feminine	
celui-ci	this one	**celle-ci**	this one
celui-là	that one	**celle-là**	that one
ceux-ci	these	**celles-ci**	these
ceux-là	those	**celles-là**	those

Examples:
Cet hôpital-ci ou celui-là?
This hospital or that one?
Quelle pharmacie préférez-vous, celle-ci ou celle-là?
Which pharmacy do you prefer, this one or that one?
Quels médicaments prenez-vous, ceux-ci ou ceux-là?
Which medicines do you take, these or those?

If you prefer not to refer to an object by name, but to call it simply "this" or "that," you can use the following:

ceci   this
cela (or **ça**)   that

Examples:
Je voudrais acheter ceci.
I'd like to buy this.
Le patient (or **la patiente**) **m'a donné cela.**
The patient gave me that.

"This," "that," "these," "those" followed by the verb "to be" are all normally translated by **c'est** or **ce sont**:

C'est votre petit déjeuner, monsieur.
This is your breakfast, sir.
Ce sont (or **c'est**) **les ordonnances que vous avez demandées.**
These are the prescriptions you asked for.

C'est, ce sont can also mean "he/she is" and "they are":

C'est un(e) dentiste (or **Il/Elle est dentiste**).
He/she is a dentist.

9

le rhume	cold
le cœur	heart
le prince	prince
la princesse	princess
le/la chirurgien(ne)	surgeon
le/la kinésithérapeute	physiotherapist
le/la pharmacien(ne)	pharmacist
le rendez-vous	appointment
la greffe	transplant
le frère/la sœur	brother/sister
le/la patient(e)	patient
moderne	modern
effectuer	to carry out

Exercise 1

Translate:

1. My cold is worse than my sister's.
2. This hospital is more modern than the one the Princess visited last year.
3. Which surgeon (m.) carried out the heart transplant? This one or that one?
4. Do you have an appointment with this dentist (m.) or that one?
5. The physiotherapist gave me this.
6. The pharmacist prepared that.
7. This is your new prescription.
8. These are your patients.

9.2 POSSESSIVE PRONOUNS: MINE, YOURS, HERS, ETC.

Instead of saying "The waiter brought your soup but not my soup," we would usually say "The waiter brought your soup but not mine." In French, the form of the possessive pronoun ("mine," "yours," "hers," etc.) must reflect the gender and number of the noun it replaces.

Pronouns replacing masculine nouns:

singular	plural	
le mien	**les miens**	mine
le tien	**les tiens**	yours (fam.)
le sien	**les siens**	his/hers
le nôtre	**les nôtres**	ours
le vôtre	**les vôtres**	yours
le leur	**les leurs**	theirs

Pronouns replacing feminine nouns:

la mienne	**les miennes**	mine
la tienne	**les tiennes**	yours (fam.)
la sienne	**les siennes**	his/hers
la nôtre	**les nôtres**	ours
la vôtre	**les vôtres**	yours
la leur	**les leurs**	theirs

Examples:
Le serveur a apporté votre soupe, mais pas la mienne.
The waiter has brought your soup, but not mine.
Voici son croissant, mais où est le vôtre?
Here's his/her croissant, but where's yours?
Notre jambon est très bon; comment est le leur?
Our ham is very good; how's theirs?
Ma bière est excellente; est-ce que la vôtre est bonne aussi?
My beer is excellent; is yours good, too?
J'ai payé mon café, mais je n'ai pas payé les leurs.
I've paid for my coffee, but I haven't paid for theirs.

9

When following the verb "to be" and having the meaning of "belonging to," the possessive pronouns are often translated by:

à moi	**à nous**
à toi	**à vous**
à lui	**à eux** (m. pl.)
à elle	**à elles** (f. pl.)

It is also possible to say **à Pierre**, **à ma femme**, etc., meaning "Pierre's," "my wife's":

Pardon, madame, est-ce que ce parapluie est à vous?
Excuse me, is this umbrella yours?
Ces gants (m.) ne sont pas à moi; ils sont à mon frère.
These gloves are not mine; they belong to my brother.

9.3 MORE QUESTION FORMS

1. "What ...?" is expressed as follows:

After a preposition, by **quoi**:

À quoi pensez-vous?
What are you thinking about?
Je pense à mon déjeuner.
I'm thinking about my lunch.
Avec quoi avez-vous payé le dîner?
What did you pay for the dinner with?
J'ai payé avec ma carte de crédit.
I paid with my credit card.

Before the verb "to be" and a noun, by **quel, quelle, quels, quelles**:

Quel est votre nom?
What is your name?
Quel est votre numéro de téléphone?
What is your telephone number?

Quelle est votre adresse?
What is your address?
Quels sont les prix?
What are the prices?

When the subject of the sentence, by **qu'est-ce qui**:

Délicieux? Qu'est-ce qui est délicieux?
Delicious? What's delicious?

When the object of the sentence, by **qu'est-ce que**
or **que (qu')**:

Qu'est-ce que vous avez comme légumes?
or **Qu'avez-vous comme légumes?**
What do you have in the way of vegetables?

As an exclamation, "What!" is translated by **Quoi!**:

Quoi! Le service n'est pas compris?
What! The service (charge) isn't included?
Quoi! Le bar est fermé?
What! The bar is closed?
Quoi! Le café n'est pas ouvert?
What! The café isn't open?

As an exclamation, "what" followed by a noun is
translated by **quel, quelle, quels, quelles**:
Quel repas! Quelle cuisinière!
What a meal! What a cook!

2. "Who, Whom ...?" is expressed as follows:

When the subject, by **qui** or **qui est-ce qui**:
Qui est-ce qui a réservé la table?
Who reserved the table?

When the object, by **qui** or **qui est-ce que**:
Qui est-ce que vous avez payé? La serveuse?
Whom did you pay? The waitress?

9

Avec qui avez-vous mangé?
Who did you eat with?

3. "Which one(s) …?" is expressed by **lequel, laquelle, lesquels, lesquelles**:

Voici trois bons vins. À votre avis, lequel est le meilleur?
Here are three good wines. In your opinion, which one is the best?
Toutes les tables sont libres, madame; laquelle préférez-vous?
All the tables are free, madam; which one do you prefer?
Des légumes? Oui, lesquels voulez-vous?
Vegetables? Yes, which would you like?

4. We saw in section 3.5 that "Which book?", "Which house?", etc. are translated as **Quel livre?**, **Quelle maison?**, etc. For example:

Quel vin avez-vous bu? Which wine did you drink?

Note that where, as in the last example, **quel** appears in a sentence with a perfect tense verb using **avoir**, the past participle must agree with it in gender and number:

Quelle viande avez-vous mangée?
Which meat did you eat?
Quels plats avez-vous recommandés?
Which dishes did you recommend?
Quelles pommes avez-vous achetées?
Which apples did you buy?

This does not apply if **quel** is preceded by a preposition:

À quelle femme avez-vous donné le livre?
Which woman did you give the book to?

5. "Whose …?" is translated by **à qui**:
À qui est ce dessert? Whose is this dessert?
À qui est cette serviette? Whose is this napkin?

9

VOCABULARY 2

le barman/ la barmaid	bartender
le whisky	whisky
le poisson	fish
le repas	meal
le couteau	knife
le chapeau	hat
la fourchette	fork
la cuillère	spoon
les baguettes (f.)	chopsticks
frais, fraîche (f.)	fresh, cool
chinois	Chinese
italien	Italian
commander	to order

IRREGULAR VERBS

sentir (to smell)

Present tense
je sens
tu sens
il/elle sent
nous sentons
vous sentez
ils/elles sentent

servir (to serve)

Present tense
je sers
tu sers
il/elle sert
nous servons
vous servez
ils/elles servent

partir (to leave)

Present tense
je pars
tu pars
il/elle part
nous partons
vous partez
ils/elles partent

9

NOTE: **payer** (to pay) is not irregular, but is a verb that has a spelling change in the stem (see section 12.5). As seen in the present tense conjugations, **y** becomes **i** before a silent **e**.

je paie	**nous payons**
tu paies	**vous payez**
il/elle paie	**ils/elles paient**

Exercise 2

Translate (use the familiar form of "you"):

1. The barman has served you your whisky, but where's mine?
2. My fish is delicious; yours is not fresh.
3. I've paid our bill and they've paid theirs.
4. Does this hat belong to you or to your friend (m.)?
5. What do you want to eat this Chinese meal with? With a knife and fork? What! No! With chopsticks.
6. What is the telephone number of the Italian restaurant?
7. Which vegetables did she order?
8. What smells so good?
9. Here's a list of the best restaurants in Paris; which one do you prefer?
10. Whose is this spoon?

9.4 MORE ADVERBS

Adverbs can be formed from adjectives ending in **-ant**, **-ent** by changing the **-nt** to **-mment**:

constant becomes **constamment** (constantly)
évident becomes **évidemment** (obviously)

Note: an important exception is **lent**, **lentement** (slowly).

A few adjectives can be used as adverbs without any change:

La soupe sent bon. The soup smells good.
Le poisson sent mauvais. The fish smells bad.
Frappez fort. Knock loudly.
Parlez plus bas. Speak more softly.

Here is a list of useful adverbs and adverbial expressions (see also section 5.4):

Time

tôt	early
tard	late
maintenant	now
tout de suite	right now
immédiatement	immediately
ensuite	afterward
toujours	always, still
hier	yesterday
aujourd'hui	today
demain	tomorrow
ce matin	this morning
cet après-midi	this afternoon
ce soir	this evening
souvent	often
rarement	rarely

Place

ici	here
là	here, there
là-bas	over there
à droite	on/to the right
à gauche	on/to the left
en haut	upstairs
en bas	downstairs
partout	everywhere

Certainty

sûrement	surely
certainement	certainly

9

Doubt

peut-être	perhaps
probablement	probably

Manner

bien	well
mal	badly
ensemble	together
surtout	especially
exprès	on purpose
vite	quickly
rapidement	rapidly
lentement	slowly
déjà	already
encore	still, yet

9.5 POSITION OF ADVERBS

In French, adverbs are placed <u>after</u> the verb, never between the subject and verb as in English:

Il parle rarement anglais.
He rarely speaks English.
Elle va souvent au théâtre.
She often goes to the theater.

In compound tenses (e.g. the perfect tenses), the following adverbs are normally placed between **avoir** (or **être**) and the past participle:

bien	**toujours**
mal	**souvent**
vite	**beaucoup**
encore	**déjà**

Examples:
Vous avez bien répondu à la question.
You have answered the question well.
Je n'ai pas encore lu votre lettre.
I haven't read your letter yet.

Votre frère est déjà parti?
Has your brother already left?

But when the adverb is an important word in the sentence, it generally comes at the end:

Je vais écrire la lettre maintenant.
I'm going to write the letter now.

VOCABULARY 3	
le bain	bath
neiger	to snow
pleuvoir	to rain

Exercise 3

Give the opposite of:

1. Ils chantent bien.
2. Ne parlez pas si fort.
3. Il va rarement chez ses parents.
4. Nous n'avons pas encore mangé.
5. Il va peut-être pleuvoir ou neiger.
6. Elle prend un bain en haut.
7. Elles feront les courses demain.

9

le mariage	wedding, marriage
le mannequin	model, dummy
la veste	jacket
la taille	size
la couleur	color
la mode	fashion
la laine	wool
la vitrine	shop window
la vente	sale
bleu marine	navy blue
gris clair	light gray
pur	pure
court	short
long, longue (f.)	long
(mal)heureusement	(un)fortunately
exactement	exactly
être en train de	to be in the middle of (doing something)
essayer	to try, to try on
ne ... que	only

IRREGULAR VERB

plaire (to please, to be pleasing: often used to express when you like something, e.g. "that pleases me")

Present tense
je plais
tu plais
il/elle plaît
nous plaisons
vous plaisez
ils/elles plaisent

Present perfect
j'ai plu, etc.

9

Une veste à la mode

CLIENT **Bonjour, madame. Je vais à un mariage la semaine prochaine ... et je voudrais acheter une veste ... une veste très chic.**

VENDEUSE **Oui, quelle est votre taille, monsieur?**

CLIENT **Je fais du 42.**

VENDEUSE **Quelle couleur préférez-vous?**

CLIENT **Je veux surtout une couleur à la mode.**

VENDEUSE **Eh bien, j'ai cette veste-ci en bleu marine en pure laine, et celle-là en gris clair.**

CLIENT **Hmm, j'aurais préféré une veste comme celle que vous avez en vitrine. Elle me plaît beaucoup.**

VENDEUSE **Malheureusement, je n'ai plus votre taille, monsieur. Je n'ai que des petites tailles.**

CLIENT **Et celle sur le mannequin, ici dans le magasin?**

VENDEUSE **C'est aussi une petite taille. Je pense qu'elle sera trop courte pour vous.**

CLIENT **Mais ... regardez! Regardez celle-là! C'est exactement ce qu'il me faut. Je vais l'essayer tout de suite.**

VENDEUSE **Non, non, non, monsieur! Cette veste-là n'est pas en vente. Elle est à ce monsieur là-bas qui est en train d'essayer un costume!**

9

A fashionable jacket

CUSTOMER Good morning. I'm going to a wedding next week … and I'd like to buy a jacket … a fashionable jacket.

SALES ASSISTANT Yes, what is your size, sir?

CUSTOMER I take size 42 [literally "I do some 42"].

SALES ASSISTANT What color do you prefer?

CUSTOMER I particularly want a color that's in fashion.

SALES ASSISTANT Well, I have this jacket in navy blue in pure wool, and that one in light gray.

CUSTOMER Hmm, I would have preferred a jacket like the one you have in the window. I like it very much [literally "It pleases me much"].

SALES ASSISTANT Unfortunately, I no longer have your size, sir. I have only small sizes.

CUSTOMER What about [literally "And"] the one which is on the model, here in the shop?

SALES ASSISTANT That's also a small size. I think it will be too short for you.

CUSTOMER But … look! Look at that one! That's exactly what I need. I'm going to try it on right away.

SALES ASSISTANT No, no, no, sir, that jacket is not for sale! It belongs to that gentleman over there who's trying on a suit!

9

Week 10

- Reflexive verbs (**se laver** "to wash oneself," as distinct from **laver** "to wash")
- Verbs preceded by prepositions
- The translation of "to" before an infinitive
- The order of pronouns
- The pronouns **en**, **y**, **on**

10.1 REFLEXIVE VERBS (**SE LAVER**)

Note the following verbs:

laver	to wash	**se laver**	to wash oneself
raser	to shave	**se raser**	to shave oneself
brûler	to burn	**se brûler**	to burn oneself
perdre	to lose	**se perdre**	to lose oneself
couper	to cut	**se couper**	to cut oneself
préparer	to prepare	**se préparer**	to prepare oneself
amuser	to amuse	**s'amuser**	to enjoy oneself
habiller	to dress	**s'habiller**	to dress oneself

The verbs in the second column are used reflexively. The present tense of a reflexive verb conjugates like this:

Present tense

je me lave	I wash myself
tu te rases	you (fam.) shave yourself
il se brûle	he burns himself
elle se prépare	she prepares herself
nous nous amusons	we enjoy ourselves
vous vous habillez	you dress yourself/yourselves
ils se perdent	they (m.) lose themselves
elles se coupent	they (f.) cut themselves

Note: **me**, **te**, and **se** become **m'**, **t'**, and **s'** before a vowel or h.

All reflexive verbs use **être** to form the perfect tenses. The past participle agrees in gender and number with the person or people performing the reflexive action.

Present perfect

je me suis lavé(e)	I washed myself
tu t'es habillé(e)	you (fam.) dressed yourself
il s'est rasé	he shaved himself
elle ne s'est pas amusée	she did not enjoy herself
nous nous sommes préparé(e)s	we prepared ourselves
vous ne vous êtes pas perdu(e)	you didn't lose yourself
vous ne vous êtes pas perdu(e)s	you didn't lose yourselves
ils se sont brûlés	they burned themselves
elles ne se sont pas coupées	they didn't cut themselves

Imperfect tense

je me lavais	I used to wash or I was washing myself

Future tense

je me laverai	I will wash myself

Conditional

je me laverais	I would wash myself

In English, we often leave out the reflexive pronoun, saying simply "I wash," "he shaves," etc. But in French, the reflexive pronoun must always be used. Compare:

Je me lave.	I'm washing (taking a bath/shower).
Je lave la voiture.	I'm washing the car.

Reflexive verbs are much more common in French than in English. Here are some that are frequently used:

se déshabiller	to undress
s'endormir	to fall asleep
se réveiller	to wake up
se lever	to get up
se dépêcher	to hurry
se promener	to go for a walk

10

se reposer	to rest
se coucher	to go to bed
se tromper	to make a mistake
s'appeler	to be called
se marier	to get married
se débarrasser de	to get rid of
se servir de	to make use of
se souvenir de	to remember

It is important to distinguish between "myself," "yourself," etc. used reflexively and the pronouns used for emphasis. Compare:

Je me lave.
I wash myself.
Je lave les enfants moi-même.
I wash the children myself.

The "-self" words used emphatically are:

moi-même	**nous-mêmes**
toi-même	**vous-même(s)**
lui-même	**eux-mêmes**
elle-même	**elles-mêmes**

VOCABULARY 1

se coiffer	to fix one's hair
se maquiller	to put on make-up
se laver les mains (f.)	to wash one's hands
se brosser les dents (f.)	to brush one's teeth

10

Exercise 1

This is what Thierry does each day.
Translate:

1. He wakes up at 7 a.m.
2. He washes.
3. He shaves.
4. He goes to work.

And now Marine:

5. She gets up at 8 a.m.
6. She takes a shower.
7. She does her hair.
8. She puts her make-up on.
9. She goes to the station.

This is what you and I do:

10. We wash.
11. We dress quickly.
12. We go for a walk.
13. We go to bed at 10 p.m.

Translate:

14. I (f.) have enjoyed myself.
15. You (f.) have not made a mistake.
16. They (f.) are resting.
17. They (m.) have washed the car themselves.
18. We brush our teeth each morning.

Reflexive pronouns are also used to convey the sense of "one another" or "each other":

Nous nous sommes souvent rencontrés.
We often met (one another).
Ils ne se comprennent pas.
They don't understand each other.

Note: In the perfect tenses, the past participle of the verb (e.g. **téléphoné**) does not agree with the number and gender of the reflexive pronoun **me**, **se**, etc. when the meaning is "to/for myself, himself," etc. Compare:

Ils se sont rencontrés. They met each other.
Ils se sont téléphoné. They called (lit. "telephoned to") each other.

10.2 VERBS PRECEDED BY PREPOSITIONS

Study the following:
1. I'm used *to getting up* very early.
2. He left *without saying* goodbye.
3. She hesitated *before replying*.
4. *After buying* a computer, he worked much more quickly.
5. These recordings are excellent *for improving* one's pronunciation.
6. He began *by criticizing* the managing director.

Note that in English, verbs preceded by a preposition end in -ing. In French, the infinitive is used:

1. **Je suis habitué à me lever très tôt.**
2. **Il est parti sans dire au revoir.**
3. **Elle a hésité avant de répondre.**
4. **Après avoir acheté un ordinateur, il a travaillé beaucoup plus vite.**
5. **Ces enregistrements sont excellents pour améliorer sa prononciation.**
6. **Il a commencé par critiquer le président-directeur général.**

10

There is one exception to this rule: the preposition **en**, which is followed by the present participle (the -ing form of the verb). More on this in section 11.4!

Also note that while in English one would usually say "after buying" etc., in French the construction has to be "after having bought" (**après avoir acheté**) or, in the case of those verbs that use **être**, **après être** ....

VOCABULARY 2

le mot	word
le ménage	housework
l'électricien(ne)	electrician
la lampe	lamp
partir	to leave
quitter	to leave (someone, somewhere)
tout le monde	everyone

Exercise 2

Translate:

1. He left the house without saying a word.
2. She's used to listening to the radio in her bedroom.
3. Before repairing the lamp, he telephoned the electrician.
4. After preparing breakfast, he did the housework.
5. My mother began by saying that the family was in good health and finished by wishing everyone a happy New Year.
6. These recordings are excellent for learning French.

Compare the following French and English sentences:

1. Je dois apprendre le français.
I have to learn French.
2. J'ai décidé d'apprendre le français.
I have decided to learn French.
3. J'ai commencé à apprendre le français.
I have started to learn French.
4. J'ai acheté ce livre pour apprendre le français.
I have bought this book to learn French.

You will see in the French sentences above that "to" before an infinitive is sometimes:

1. not translated
2. translated by **de (d')**
3. translated by **à**
4. translated by **pour**

Unfortunately, there is only one case in which it is pretty clear which preposition to use: when "to" means "in order to," use **pour**.

The rest of the time, it's a question of learning through practice which verbs take no preposition, which take **de**, and which take **à**.

Here are some verbs for each case, followed by a few model sentences as examples.

"To" is not translated before an infinitive after these verbs:

aimer	to like, to love
préférer	to prefer
vouloir	to want
désirer/souhaiter	to wish, to want
aller	to go
venir	to come

10

devoir	to have to
falloir (il faut)	to be necessary
espérer	to hope
pouvoir	to be able
savoir	to know how

"To" is translated by **de** before an infinitive after these verbs:

cesser	to stop
conseiller	to advise
décider	to decide
demander	to ask
dire	to tell
empêcher	to prevent
essayer	to try
éviter	to avoid
finir	to finish
oublier	to forget
permettre	to allow
persuader	to persuade
promettre	to promise
proposer	to propose
refuser	to refuse
regretter	to regret

Note also:

être content de	to be pleased to
être heureux de	to be happy to
être ravi de	to be delighted to
être triste de	to be sad to
être désolé de	to be sorry to
avoir l'intention de	to intend to
avoir l'occasion de	to have the opportunity to
avoir le temps de	to have the time to
avoir le plaisir de	to have the pleasure to
il est facile de	it is easy to
il est difficile de	it is difficult to
il est possible de	it is possible to
il est impossible de	it is impossible to
il est permis de	it is permitted to

il est interdit de	it is forbidden to
il est temps de	it is time to

"To" is translated by **à** before an infinitive following these verbs:

aider	to help
apprendre	to learn
avoir	to have
commencer	to begin
continuer	to continue
encourager	to encourage
enseigner	to teach
hésiter	to hesitate
inviter	to invite
réussir	to succeed

Note also:

être prêt à	to be ready to
être disposé à	to be willing to
avoir de la difficulté à	to have difficulty in
avoir du mal à	to have difficulty in

Examples:

Je préfère aller me baigner.
I prefer to go for a swim.

Nous espérons aller à la plage cet après-midi.
We hope to go to the beach this afternoon.

Ils ont décidé de louer un pédalo.
They have decided to hire a pedal boat.

Je vous conseille de faire une promenade en bateau.
I advise you to go on a boat trip.

Nous sommes contents de voir le soleil.
We are pleased to see the sun.

Avez-vous réussi à trouver des chaises longues?
Did you succeed in finding some deckchairs?

Nous l'avons aidée à chercher des coquillages (m.).
We helped her look for some shells.

Il est temps de rentrer à l'hôtel.
It's time to return to the hotel.

10

Exercise 3

Complete the following:

1. (I intend to) acheter des lunettes de soleil.
2. (Will it be possible to) faire des excursions?
3. (We prefer to) louer un appartement.
4. (They [m.] invited me [f.] to) aller à la pêche.
5. (I hesitate to) faire du ski nautique.
6. (Will you have the opportunity to) faire de la planche à voile?

10.4 ORDER OF PRONOUNS ("HE GAVE IT TO ME")

In sentences such as "he gave it to him" or "I'm sending them to you," a different word order is used in French. Notice that **le**, **la**, **l'**, **les** follow **me**, **vous**, **nous**:

Paul me le donne. Paul gives it (m.) to me.
Nicole nous la vend. Nicole sells it (f.) to us.
Je vous les enverrai. I'll send them to you.

But **le**, **la**, **l'**, **les** precede **lui** and **leur**:

Nous le lui avons déjà montré.
We have already shown it (m.) to him (or to her).
Vous la leur avez donnée?
Did you give it (f.) to them?
Je ne les lui ai pas vendus.
I didn't sell them to him (or to her).

VOCABULARY 4

le dossier	file
le/la collègue	colleague
le mail	email
la moto	motorcycle
la facture	invoice

Exercise 4

Replace all nouns with pronouns (and make any necessary changes):

1. Est-ce que vous m'avez donné le dossier?
2. Notre directeur nous a promis les deux voitures.
3. Mon collègue a l'intention de me vendre ses livres.
4. J'ai envoyé un mail à Omar.
5. Raphaël montre sa nouvelle moto à Vincent.
6. Nous avons donné les factures aux clients.

10

10.5 USEFUL PRONOUNS: EN

The pronoun **en** replaces a word or an idea introduced by
de. It can mean:

1. "Some" or "any," when not followed by a noun:

Avez-vous des journaux américains?
Do you have any American newspapers?
Oui, nous en avons.
Yes, we have some.
Non, nous n'en avons pas.
No, we don't have any.

Note that "some," "any" must be expressed in French,
even when they can be omitted in English:

Avez-vous des enveloppes (f.)?
Do you have any envelopes?
Oui, j'en ai. Yes, I have.

2. "Of it," "of them":

As-tu acheté des fruits?
Did you buy any fruit?
Oui, j'en ai acheté beaucoup.
Yes, I bought a lot (of it).
Ont-ils des enfants?
Do they have any children?
Oui, ils en ont deux.
Yes, they have two (of them).

3. "About it," "about them":

Avez-vous parlé de la navette spatiale?
Did you talk about ("of") the space shuttle?
Oui, tous les astronautes en parlent!
Yes, all the astronauts are talking about it!

10

4. "From there":

Est-ce que les ingénieurs vont au centre de contrôle?
Are the engineers going to the control center?
Non, ils en viennent.
No, they've just come (lit. "they come") from there.

10.6 USEFUL PRONOUNS: Y

The pronoun **y** replaces a word or an idea introduced by
à. It can mean:

1. "There":

Est-ce que Paul connaît les Etats-Unis?
Does Paul know the United States?
Oui, il y a passé trois ans.
Yes, he spent three years there.
Est-ce que tu viens de la gare?
Are you coming from the station?
Non, j'y vais.
No, I'm going there.

Note: when actually pointing, use **là** or **là-bas** for "there."

2. "To it," "to them":

Il faut toujours faire la queue à cette boulangerie.
One always has to stand in line at this bakery.
Oui, mais les clients y sont habitués.
Yes, but the customers are used to it.

Note that **y** cannot be omitted:

Est-ce que le directeur est dans son bureau?
Is the director in his office?
Oui, il y est.
Yes, he is.

10

In English, when referring to people in general, words such as "we," "they," "you," "people" are used: e.g. "In Britain, we drive on the left" or "In China, they eat with chopsticks." In this case, the pronoun **on** (the equivalent of "one") is used in French with the third-person singular verb (the **il** or **elle** conjugation):

En Angleterre, on roule à gauche.
In England, they drive on the left.
En Chine, on mange avec des baguettes.
In China, they eat with chopsticks.
On dit qu'il parle sept langues.
People say he speaks seven languages.

On is often used to translate the English passive voice:

On a invité les diplomates chinois à l'Ambassade de France.
The Chinese diplomats have been invited to the French Embassy.

Informally in conversation, the French very often use **on** in place of **nous**:

Alors, on va partir aujourd'hui ou demain?
Well, are we going to leave today or tomorrow?

Note: **on** sometimes becomes **l'on** after **et** and **si**; the French find this a more flowing liaison.

10

le banc	bench
l'attitude (f.)	attitude
la promotion	promotion
la chance	luck
l'enceinte (f.) connectée	smart speaker
sociable	sociable
récemment	recently
encore	again
bien sûr	of course
alors	well
lorsque	when
perfectionner	to perfect
apprécier	to appreciate
s'acheter	to buy for oneself

IRREGULAR VERBS

s'asseoir (to sit down)

Present tense
je m'assieds
tu t'assieds
il/elle/on s'assied
nous nous asseyons
vous vous asseyez
ils/elles s'asseyent

Present perfect
je me suis assis(e), etc.

Future tense
je m'assiérai, etc.

obtenir (to obtain, to get)

Present tense
j'obtiens
tu obtiens
il/elle/on obtient
nous obtenons
vous obtenez
ils/elles obtiennent

Present perfect
j'ai obtenu, etc.

Future tense
j'obtiendrai, etc.

sortir (to go out)

Present tense
je sors
tu sors
il/elle/on sort

nous sortons
vous sortez
ils/elles sortent

10

L'anglais en trois mois

DAVID Est-ce que vous vous servez toujours de la chaîne hi-fi que vous avez achetée il y a quelques années?

ISABELLE Non, je ne me sers plus de celle-là. Je m'en suis débarrassée et je me suis acheté une enceinte connectée beaucoup plus perfectionnée.

DAVID N'est-il pas difficile d'apprécier la musique avec un si petit appareil?

ISABELLE Vous vous trompez, ce n'est pas de la musique que j'écoute, ce sont des cours d'anglais. Je les ai achetés parce que je dois apprendre l'anglais en trois mois.

DAVID Est-ce que vous avez le temps d'écouter ces enregistrements?

ISABELLE Oui, bien sûr. Je les écoute le matin lorsque je me lave, lorsque je m'habille, lorsque je me coiffe et lorsque je me maquille. Mon mari les écoute aussi quand il se rase, quand il se lave et se brosse les dents. Le dimanche nous aimons sortir et je les écoute encore lorsque nous nous promenons au parc et lorsque nous nous asseyons sur un banc pour nous reposer.

DAVID Ce n'est pas une attitude très sociable.

ISABELLE C'est vrai, mais si je réussis à apprendre l'anglais en trois mois, il me sera possible d'obtenir une promotion et de partir en Angleterre et aux États-Unis.

DAVID Bon, alors, bonne chance ou, comme on dit en anglais, "good luck"!

10

English in three months

DAVID   Are you still using the hi-fi you bought a few years ago?

ISABELLE   No, I'm not using that anymore. I got rid of it and I've bought myself a much more sophisticated [literally "perfected"] smart speaker.

DAVID   Isn't it difficult to appreciate music with such a small device?

ISABELLE   You're mistaken, it's not music I listen to, it's English-language courses [literally "courses of English"]. I bought them because I have to learn English in three months.

DAVID   Do you have the time to listen to these recordings?

ISABELLE   Yes, of course. I listen to them in the morning when I'm washing, when I'm getting dressed, when I'm doing my hair, and when I'm putting on my make-up. My husband also listens to them when he's shaving, when he's washing, and brushing his teeth. On Sundays, we like to go out and I listen to them again when we're walking in the park and when we sit down on a bench for a rest.

DAVID   That's not a very sociable attitude.

ISABELLE   That's true, but if I succeed in learning English in three months, it will be possible for me to get a promotion and leave for England and the United States.

DAVID   Good, well, good luck or, as they say in English, "good luck"!

10

Week 11

Conjunctions: words such as "because" and "while" that join parts of a sentence together
Numbers over 100
The passive voice
The present participle (the -ing form)
More about the imperative
The past perfect ("I had spoken," etc.)
*Using **depuis** ("since") and **venir de** ("to have just ...")*

11.1 CONJUNCTIONS: BUT, BECAUSE, WHILE, ETC.

The following are some frequently used conjunctions:

Reason
parce que	because
car	for, because
puisque	since
comme	as, since
donc	so, therefore

Time
quand	when
lorsque	when
dès que	as soon as
aussitôt que	as soon as
pendant que	while
maintenant que	now that

Contrast
mais	but
tandis que	whereas

Examples:
Nous avons acheté une tente, car nous voulons faire du camping.
We bought a tent because we want to go camping.

Mon père n'aime pas l'Italie, donc nous sommes allés en Allemagne.
My father doesn't like Italy, so we went to Germany.
Puisque tu es fatigué, nous pourrions camper ici.
Since you're tired, we could camp here.
Pendant que tu vas chercher de la bière, je vais regarder la télévision.
While you go and get some beer, I'll watch television.
C'est un bon camping, mais où sont les toilettes?
It's a good campsite, but where are the toilets?

Note that you must use the future tense after **quand**, **lorsque**, **dès que**, and **aussitôt que** when the future is referred to:

Quand nous ferons du camping l'année prochaine, toute la famille s'amusera bien.
When we go camping next year, the whole family will have a good time.
Aussitôt que tu seras prêt, je préparerai à manger.
As soon as you're ready, I'll prepare something to eat.

BUT not if "when" means "whenever":

Quand je suis en vacances, je dépense toujours beaucoup d'argent.
When I'm on vacation, I always spend a lot of money.

VOCABULARY 1

le sac de couchage	sleeping bag
le champ	field
la piscine	swimming pool
supplémentaire	extra
tomber en panne	to break down

11

Exercise 1

Translate:

1. As Paul's friend (m.) is coming camping with us, we'll have to buy an extra sleeping bag.

2. When you (pl.) can speak French, we'll go camping in France.

3. Do you take every opportunity to speak French when you're in Belgium?

4. I don't like this campsite because there's no swimming pool.

5. There are four of us (say "We are four"), but we only have three sleeping bags.

6. The car broke down, so we decided to camp in a field.

11.2 NUMBERS OVER 100

Here are the numbers between a hundred and a million:

100	cent
101	cent un
110	cent dix
150	cent cinquante
200	deux cents
300	trois cents
400	quatre cents
520	cinq cent vingt
640	six cent quarante
750	sept cent cinquante
800	huit cents
960	neuf cent soixante
1,000	mille
1,250	mille deux cent cinquante
2,000	deux mille
8,000	huit mille
9,000	neuf mille
1,000,000	un million

11

NOTE:
• **Cent** drops the **s** when followed by another number:
trois cents livres BUT **trois cent quarante livres**

• When followed by a noun, **un million** takes **de**:
un million de dollars

• In dates, **mille** is sometimes written **mil**:
en mille (or **mil) neuf cent quatre-vingt-seize**

Ordinal numbers (first, second, etc.) are formed like this:

1st	**premier**	8th	**huitième**
2nd	**deuxième**	9th	**neuvième**
3rd	**troisième**	10th	**dixième**
4th	**quatrième**	20th	**vingtième**
5th	**cinquième**	21st	**vingt et unième**
6th	**sixième**	22nd	**vingt-deuxième**
7th	**septième**		

NOTE:
• **Premier** has a feminine form: **première**
• **Deuxième** has an alternative: **second, seconde (f.)**
• The spelling of **cinquième** and **neuvième**
• In French, instead of "Louis the Fourteenth," it is
"Louis fourteen": **Louis quatorze, Henri huit**, etc.

Exercise 2

Complete the following, writing the answers in full:

A. 150 + 100 =   **D.** 450 + 120 =

B. 260 + 40 =   **E.** 580 + 100 =

C. 320 + 110 =   **F.** 1,000 + 440 =

11

Exercise 3

Translate:

1. the first party
2. the second performance
3. the third night club
4. the fourth theater
5. the fifth concert
6. the sixth opera
7. the seventh cinema
8. the eighth skating rink
9. the ninth ballet
10. the tenth restaurant

11.3 THE PASSIVE VOICE

As in English, the passive is formed with the verb "to be," **être**, and the past participle, e.g. **fait** (done). The past participle agrees with the subject; "by" is translated by **par**:

Un tunnel sera construit l'année prochaine.
A tunnel will be built next year.

Le traité a été signé par les deux gouvernements.

The treaty has been signed by both governments.

While "by" is usually translated as **par**, it may also be **de**, especially after verbs of feeling. Note also that the past participle changes to reflect the gender and number of the subject of the sentence:

Cette experte est respectée de tout le monde.
This expert is respected by everyone.

However, there is a tendency in French to avoid the passive in one of the following ways:

1. By using the pronoun **on** (see section 10.7):

On a déjà oublié qu'il y a dix ans, il n'y avait pas de grands arbres dans la ville.
It has already been forgotten that ten years ago, there were no big trees in the city.

The use of **on** is essential in the case of verbs after which the preposition "to" is used or implied—**donner à** (to give to), **dire à** (to tell, to say to), **répondre à** (to reply to, to answer), **demander à** (to ask). Although in English you can say "I've been given," "he's been told," "the letter has been answered," "she's been asked," and so on, this construction is impossible in French. You must use **on**:

On m'a dit qu'il y aura un train toutes les trois minutes.
I've been told there will be a train every three minutes.
On lui a demandé ce qu'il pensait du projet.
He was asked what he thought of the project.
On a déjà répondu à la lettre.
The letter has already been answered.

2. By using the active voice instead:

La construction de ce pont a créé beaucoup d'emplois.
Many jobs have been created by the building of the bridge.

11

3. Occasionally by using a reflexive verb:

Cela ne se vend pas en France.
That's not sold in France.

VOCABULARY 3

le continent	continent
la traversée	crossing
la république	republic
la décision	decision
l'importance (f.)	importance
ferroviaire	rail
routier, routière (f.)	road (adj.)
historique	historic
étranger, étrangère (f.)	foreign
relier	to link
annoncer	to announce
souligner	to emphasize, to underline

IRREGULAR VERB

construire (to build)

Present tense
je construis
tu construis
il/elle/on construit
nous construisons
vous construisez
ils/elles construisent

Present tense
j'ai construit, etc.

11

Exercise 4

Britain and France made the decision to build the Channel Tunnel in 1986. Read the following sentences, taken from a newspaper article published at the time. Then change them into the passive:

1. Le président de la République française a souligné l'importance de la décision.
2. Un tunnel ferroviaire reliera la Grande-Bretagne au continent en 1993.
3. On construira plus tard un lien routier.
4. On a annoncé cette décision historique à Lille.
5. La traversée de la Manche a souvent découragé les touristes étrangers.

11.4 THE PRESENT PARTICIPLE

The present participle in English ends in -ing, and it is often preceded by "while," "on," "by," or "in." In French, it ends in **-ant** and is often preceded by **en**:

Il s'est cassé la jambe, en jouant au football.
He broke his leg while playing soccer (football).
En étudiant un peu tous les jours, vous apprendrez le français en trois mois.
By studying a little every day, you will learn French in three months.

As in English, the present participle can also be used without a preceding preposition:

Voyant que le patron était de bonne humeur, il a demandé une augmentation de salaire.
Seeing that the boss was in a good mood, he asked for an increase in salary.

11

The present participle is formed by removing the ending **-ons** from the first-person plural of the present tense and adding **-ant**:

chantant   singing
finissant   finishing
vendant   selling
écrivant   writing

There are three exceptions: **avoir**, **être**, and **savoir**.

ayant   having
étant   being
sachant   knowing

Remember that **en** is the only preposition that is followed by the present participle in French; all others are followed by the infinitive (see section 10.2).

Remember also that sentences such as "I am going," "I am watching," "I am listening" are translated by the present tense (see section 2.3):

je vais   I'm going
je regarde   I'm watching
j'écoute   I'm listening

11

VOCABULARY 4

le bras	arm
le cours	course, class
le diplôme	diploma
le policier/	police officer
la policière	
la fois	time, occasion
la réponse	reply
blessé	injured
par	per, by
faire du ski	to ski
faire du roller	to rollerblade
tomber	to fall (conjugated with **être**)
appeler	to call (see section 12.5)

IRREGULAR VERB

voir (to see)

Present tense
je vois
tu vois
il/elle/on voit
nous voyons
vous voyez
ils/elles voient

Present perfect
j'ai vu, etc.

Future tense
je verrai, etc.

Exercise 5

Combine the following using a present participle:

1. Elle s'est cassé le bras. Elle faisait du ski.
2. Je suis tombé. Je faisais du roller.
3. Il allait aux cours du soir trois fois par semaine. Il a obtenu son diplôme.
4. Le policier a vu que le conducteur était blessé. Il a appelé les secours.
5. Vous téléphonez. Vous aurez la réponse tout de suite.

11

11.5 MORE ABOUT THE IMPERATIVE

The imperative (command form) of **avoir** and **être** is:

aie	have (fam.)	**sois**	be (fam.)
ayez	have	**soyez**	be
ayons	let's have	**soyons**	let's be

Examples:
Ayez un peu de patience. Have a little patience.
Ne soyez pas en retard. Don't be late.
Soyons raisonnables. Let's be reasonable.

11.6 THE IMPERATIVE WITH PRONOUNS

Read through these examples of the imperative:

Invitez votre collègue au restaurant.
Invite your colleague to the restaurant.
Invitez-la.
Invite her.
Ne l'invitez pas.
Don't invite her.

Donnez le numéro de téléphone aux clients.
Give the telephone number to the clients.
Donnez-leur le numéro.
Give them the number.
Ne leur donnez pas le numéro.
Don't give them the number.

Asseyez-vous dans ce fauteuil.
Sit down in this armchair.
Ne vous asseyez pas dans ce fauteuil.
Don't sit down in this armchair.

Note that a pronoun follows the verb in the affirmative imperative, while it precedes the verb in the negative imperative.

11

Here are some other examples:

Donnez-moi votre adresse.
Give me your address.
Donnez-la-moi.
Give it to me.
Ne me donnez pas votre adresse.
Don't give me your address.
Ne me la donnez pas.
Don't give it to me.
Couche-toi.
Lie down.
Ne te couche pas.
Don't lie down.

Note that **me** and **te** become **moi** and **toi** in the affirmative imperative, and note the word order in **donnez-le-moi, envoyez-la-moi, montrez-les-moi**.

If you want to make a request more polite, instead of using the imperative, you can phrase it as a question using one of the following expressions in front of the infinitive:

Voulez-vous ...?	Will you ...?
Voulez-vous bien ...?	Would you kindly ...?
Pourriez-vous ...?	Could you ...?

Examples:
Voulez-vous signer ici, s'il vous plaît?
Will you sign here, please?
Voulez-vous bien passer à la caisse, s'il vous plaît?
Would you kindly go to the cash register/checkout, please?
Pourriez-vous nous apporter encore du café?
Could you bring us some more coffee?

11

VOCABULARY 5

le catalogue	catalog
l'échantillon (m.)	sample
la brochure	brochure
faire des heures (f.) **supplémentaires**	to work overtime

Exercise 6

Imagine you're asking your personal assistant to carry out a number of tasks. The trouble is you keep changing your mind!

Translate:

1. Telephone him—no, don't telephone him.
2. Send them this brochure—no, don't send it to them.
3. Copy this document—no, don't copy it.
4. Give me the catalog—no, don't give it to me.
5. Send her the samples—no, don't send them to her.
6. Be here at 9 o'clock—no, at 8 o'clock.
7. Would you be so kind as to work overtime?

11.7 THE PAST PERFECT ("HE HAD GONE")

The past perfect ("I had telephoned," "I had spoken," etc.) is expressed using the imperfect of **avoir** or **être** with the past participle:

J'avais déjà téléphoné à l'hôpital.
I had already called the hospital.
Elle était déjà partie, quand son mari est arrivé.
She had already left when her husband arrived.

11

11.8 DEPUIS ("SINCE")

In French, the present tense is sometimes used when we would use the present perfect tense in English. This is the case when an action that began in the past is still continuing into the present:

Depuis quand êtes-vous en France?
How long have you been in France? (lit. "Since when are you in France?")
Depuis combien de temps apprenez-vous le français?
How long have you been learning French?
Je suis en France depuis une semaine, mais j'apprends le français depuis trois mois.
I've been in France for a week, but I've been learning French for three months.

11.9 VENIR DE ("TO HAVE JUST ...")

This idiomatic expression, used only in the present and imperfect tenses, expresses the idea of "having just done something":

Je viens d'acheter une maison.
I have just bought a house.
Elle venait de vendre son appartement.
She had just sold her apartment.

11

VOCABULARY 6

les secours	rescue service
les pompiers	firefighters
l'ambulance (f.)	ambulance
le permis de conduire	driver's license
jouer du piano	to play the piano
prévenir	to inform (conjugates like **venir**)
transporter	to transport

Exercise 7

Translate:

1. I've been married for five years.
2. I've lived in this house for four years.
3. I've worked for this bank for three years.
4. I've had this car for two years.
5. I've been learning to play the piano for one year.

Exercise 8

Answer the questions as follows:

Allez-vous téléphoner à la police?
　　Are you going to call the police?

Mais je viens de téléphoner à la police.
　　But I've just called the police.

1. Allez-vous appeler un docteur?
2. Allez-vous prévenir les pompiers?
3. Pouvez-vous me montrer votre permis de conduire?
4. Est-ce que les ambulances vont transporter les blessés à l'hôpital?
5. Est-ce que vous allez me donner votre adresse?

le volant	steering wheel
l'isolement (m.)	isolation
la fin	end
l'île (f.)	island
la façon	way, manner
de toutes façons	anyway, in any case
faciliter	to facilitate, to make easy
construire	to build
l'entente (f.)	understanding
nécessaire	necessary
contre	against
cordial	cordial
jurer	to swear
Vive …!	Long live …!

IRREGULAR VERB

vivre (to live)

Present tense
je vis
tu vis
il/elle/on vit
nous vivons
vous vivez
ils/elles vivent

Present perfect
j'ai vécu, etc.

11

Le tunnel sous la Manche

Une conversation entre un Anglais et une Française

FRANÇAISE **On dit que le tunnel sous la Manche est un vrai succès pour nos deux pays. Qu'en pensez-vous?**

ANGLAIS **Oui, c'est vrai. Mais pourqui construire un tunnel ferroviaire? Quand Mme Thatcher était Premier ministre britannique, elle avait juré qu'elle serait la première à traverser la Manche au volant de sa voiture.**

FRANÇAISE **C'est possible, mais elle n'est plus Premier ministre depuis longtemps. De toutes façons, les voitures utilisent le train pour traverser la Manche, avec le Shuttle. Ça marche bien, je trouve. Qu'est-ce que vous pensez vous-même du tunnel?**

ANGLAIS **Eh bien, en construisant ce tunnel, on a mis fin à l'isolement de la Grande-Bretagne, et en même temps on a créé de nouveaux emplois.**

FRANÇAISE **Y a-t-il donc des gens qui sont contre le tunnel?**

ANGLAIS **Oui, il y a des gens qui pensent que la Grande-Bretagne aurait dû rester une île. Je ne suis pas sûr qu'ils aient raison.**

FRANÇAISE **De toutes façons, avec un tunnel ou sans tunnel—vive l'Entente cordiale!**

11

The Tunnel under the Channel

A conversation between an Englishman and a Frenchwoman

FRENCHWOMAN It is said that the Channel Tunnel has been a real success for both our countries. What do you think?

ENGLISHMAN Yes, it's true. But why a rail tunnel? When Mrs. Thatcher was British Prime Minister, she swore that she would be the first to cross the Channel at the wheel of her car.

FRENCHWOMAN Yes, but she hasn't been Prime Minister for a long time. In any case, cars use the train to cross the Channel with the Shuttle. It works well, I find. What do you yourself think of the tunnel?

ENGLISHMAN Well, by building the tunnel, we have put an end to Britain's isolation, and at the same time we have created new jobs.

FRENCHWOMAN Are there people who are against the Tunnel?

ENGLISHMAN Yes, there are people who think that Great Britain should have remained an island. I am not sure they're right.

FRENCHWOMAN Anyway, with a tunnel or without a tunnel— long live the Entente Cordiale!

11

Week 12

- The many uses of **faire**
- The past historic tense (regular and irregular verbs)
- Verbs needing/not needing a preposition
- Spelling changes in verbs (to keep them regular)
- The subjunctive mood, used to express what is imagined, wished, or possible rather than factual

12.1 THE MANY USES OF THE VERB **FAIRE**

Arguably, **faire** is one of the most overworked verbs in the French language. It conjugates as follows:

Present tense
je fais
tu fais
il/elle/on fait
nous faisons
vous faites
ils/elles font

Present perfect
j'ai fait, etc.

Imperfect
je faisais, etc.

Future
je ferai, etc.

The verb **faire** can have a variety of meanings, as shown in the following examples:

to do:
Qu'est-ce que vous faites dans la vie?
What do you do for a living?

to make:
Ma mère va faire un gâteau.
My mother is going to make a cake.

to give:
Je vais faire une conférence sur l'énergie renouvelable.
I'm going to give a lecture on renewable energy.

to take:
Elle aime faire une promenade au parc.
She likes to take a walk in the park.

to have:
Mon mari fait de la tension.
My husband has high blood pressure.

to act:
Ne fais pas l'idiot.
Don't act the fool.

to force:
Je l'ai fait travailler.
I forced him to work (or I made him work).

to have something done:
Ils font construire une maison.
They're having a house built.

You'll find **faire** in various expressions used to talk about the weather (see section 6.8):
Il fait beau.
The weather is fine.

It is also used in many idiomatic expressions:
Tu me fais marcher.
You're pulling my leg.

12

VOCABULARY 1

la profession	profession
la tarte	tart
la pomme	apple
la psychologie	psychology
la fièvre	fever
bête	silly

Exercise 1

Rewrite the following using the verb faire:

1. Quelle est votre profession?
2. Ma sœur prépare une tarte aux pommes.
3. Je vais parler de la psychologie devant 200 personnes.
4. Elle s'est promenée au parc hier.
5. Il a de la fièvre.
6. Ne sois pas bête.
7. J'ai forcé mon fils à travailler.
8. On me construit une maison à Avignon.

12.2 THE PAST HISTORIC

There is a past tense that you might come across in written language but is almost never used in conversation: the past historic (or past definite). It is a literary tense, and you will never need to use it, but it is useful to be able to recognize it.

The past historic describes a completed action that occurred in the past and, in the case of regular verbs, is formed by removing the **-er**, **-ir**, **-re** from the infinitive and adding the conjugation endings as follows.

12

-er verbs		-ir/-re verbs	
je	-ai	je	-is
tu	-as	tu	-is
il/elle	-a	il/elle	-it
nous	-âmes	nous	-îmes
vous	-âtes	vous	-îtes
ils/elles	-èrent	ils/elles	-irent

Examples:

Le lendemain Paul arriva tôt.
The following day, Paul arrived early.
Les touristes visitèrent cinq pays en cinq jours.
The tourists visited five countries in five days.
Victor Hugo finit d'écrire *Les Misérables* en 1862.
Victor Hugo finished writing *Les Misérables* in 1862.

12.3 THE PAST HISTORIC OF IRREGULAR VERBS

You will sometimes be able to recognize the past historic of irregular verbs by the similarity to the past participle:

Infinitive	Present perfect	Past historic	Meaning
dire	**j'ai dit**	**je dis**	I said
mettre	**j'ai mis**	**je mis**	I put
prendre	**j'ai pris**	**je pris**	I took
sortir	**je suis sorti**	**je sortis**	I went out
avoir	**j'ai eu**	**j'eus**	I had
lire	**j'ai lu**	**je lus**	I read
vivre	**j'ai vécu**	**je vécus**	I lived

Other irregular forms just have to be learned:

Infinitive	Present perfect	Past historic	Meaning
écrire	**j'ai écrit**	**j'écrivis**	I wrote
être	**j'ai été**	**je fus**	I was
faire	**j'ai fait**	**je fis**	I did
venir	**je suis venu**	**je vins**	I came
voir	**j'ai vu**	**je vis**	I saw

12

Exercise 2

Translate into English:

1. Il donna.
2. Je vendis.
3. Nous finîmes.
4. Elle eut.
5. Je fus.
6. Vous eûtes.
7. Il prit.
8. Elle sortit.
9. Ils lurent.
10. Elles mirent.

12.4 VERBS WITH OR WITHOUT A PREPOSITION

Although a preposition is necessary in English to complete the meaning of the following verbs, none is required in French:

to approve of	**approuver**
to listen to	**écouter**
to look at	**regarder**
to look for	**chercher**
to ask for	**demander**
to pay for	**payer**
to wait for	**attendre**

Conversely, a preposition is sometimes needed with a French verb, but not in English:

demander à	to ask
dire à	to tell
défendre à	to forbid
obéir à	to obey
permettre à	to allow
ressembler à	to resemble
toucher à	to touch
jouer à	to play (a game)
jouer de	to play (an instrument)

Examples:
J'ai écouté les explications du guide avec attention.
I listened carefully to the guide's explanations.

Regardez la cathédrale à droite.
Look at the cathedral on the right.
Attendez les autres membres du groupe.
Wait for the other members of the group.
Nous cherchons les toilettes.
We are looking for the toilets.
Je vais demander deux billets d'entrée.
I'm going to ask for two admission tickets.
Il aime jouer au tennis.
He likes to play tennis.
Elle aime jouer du piano.
She likes to play the piano.

12.5 SPELLING CHANGES

In certain French verbs, the different conjugations require spelling changes so that the basic sound of the verb remains unchanged. Let's take the example of the commonly used verb **manger** (to eat).

We've learned that the present tense is formed by removing the ending of the infinitive (e.g. -**er**) and adding the conjugation ending. For example, in the case of **nous**, we add -**ons**. But if we do this with the verb **manger**, pronounced "mah*ng*-zhay," we would have "**mangons**," pronounced "mah*ng*-gon*g*" i.e. a change in the basic sound. So in order to keep the soft sound "zh," an **e** must be added: **nous mangeons**. This spelling change occurs whenever the **g** is followed by **o** or **a**:

nous mangeons	we eat	(present tense)
je mangeais	I was eating	(imperfect)
il mangea	he ate	(past historic)
en mangeant	while eating	(present participle)

Here are some important verbs that behave like **manger**:

arranger	to arrange
corriger	to correct
décourager	to discourage

12

encourager	to encourage
déranger	to disturb
nager	to swim
voyager	to travel

This change in order to retain the soft **g** also applies to the soft **c** in a verb such as **annoncer** (to announce). To keep the soft **c** in the **nous** form, we have to add a cedilla to the **c**: **nous annonçons**. Otherwise, the pronunciation would be "ah-no*ng*-ko*ng*." So there is a spelling change of **ç** before **o** and **a**:

nous annonçons	we announce
j'annonçais	I was announcing
il annonça	he announced
en annonçant	while announcing

Some other verbs with the same spelling change:

commencer	to begin
divorcer	to divorce
prononcer	to pronounce
remplacer	to replace

Some verbs that have an infinitive ending in **-eler** or **-eter** double the **l** or **t** before a silent **e**:

appeler (to call)

Present tense

j'appelle	**nous appelons**
tu appelles	**vous appelez**
il/elle appelle	**ils/elles appellent**

Future tense
j'appellerai

Conditional
j'appellerais

12

Some other verbs like **appeler**:

rappeler	to call back, to remind
renouveler	to renew
jeter	to throw

Some verbs change **e** to **è** before a silent **e**:

acheter (to buy)

Present tense

j'achète	**nous achetons**
tu achètes	**vous achetez**
il/elle achète	**ils/elles achètent**

Future tense
j'achèterai

Conditional
j'achèterais

Some other verbs like **acheter**:

lever	to raise
se lever	to get up
mener	to lead
amener	to bring

Some verbs change **é** to **è** before a silent **e** (present tense and present subjunctive only):

espérer (to hope)

Present tense

j'espère	**nous espérons**
tu espères	**vous espérez**
il/elle espère	**ils/elles espèrent**

Some other verbs like **espérer**:

considérer	to consider

12

régler	to settle
répéter	to repeat
s'inquiéter	to worry
préférer	to prefer

Verbs that have an infinitive ending in **-yer** change **y** to **i** before a silent **e**:

nettoyer (to clean)

Present tense

je nettoie	**nous nettoyons**
tu nettoies	**vous nettoyez**
il/elle nettoie	**ils/elles nettoient**

Future tense
je nettoierai

Conditional
je nettoierais

Some other verbs like **nettoyer**:

employer	to use
s'ennuyer	to be bored
envoyer	to send (future: **j'enverrai**)
payer	to pay (optional spelling change)
essayer	to try (optional spelling change)

12.6 THE SUBJUNCTIVE

There is a subjunctive mood in English, although it is used far less often than in French. In English, when we make a suggestion or express a wish, we use the subjunctive. For example, when we say "I suggest that a vote be taken" or "I wish today were Saturday," "be" and "were" are in the subjunctive.

In French, the subjunctive is used after verbs and expressions that denote:

12

a wish	**vouloir, désirer**	to want, to wish
a preference	**préférer**	to prefer
a suggestion	**suggérer, proposer**	to suggest
a necessity	**falloir**	to be necessary
a demand	**exiger**	to demand
surprise	**être surpris**	to be surprised
regret	**regretter**	to regret
anger	**être furieux**	to be furious
fear	**avoir peur**	to be afraid
doubt	**douter**	to doubt
possibility	**être possible**	to be possible
pleasure	**être content**	to be pleased
sorrow	**être désolé**	to be sorry

The subjunctive is always preceded by **que** (that). It is formed by removing the **-ent** ending from the third-person plural form of the present tense and adding:

je	-e	**nous**	-ions
tu	-es	**vous**	-iez
il/elle	-e	**ils/elles**	-ent

Examples:

... que je parle	**... que nous vendions**
... que tu donnes	**... que vous répondiez**
... qu'il finisse	**... qu'ils mettent**
... qu'elle maigrisse	**... qu'elles permettent**

Examples of the use of the subjunctive:
Je voudrais que vous me fixiez un rendez-vous chez le coiffeur.
I would like you to fix an appointment for me at the hairdresser.
Je voudrais que vous me coupiez les cheveux.
I would like you to cut my hair.
Je préfère qu'il ne me coupe pas les cheveux trop court.
I prefer him not to cut my hair too short.
Je veux qu'il me fasse un brushing.
I want him to blow-dry my hair.

12

Il faut que vous me mettiez un peu de laque (f.) sur les cheveux à cause du vent.
You must put a little hairspray on my hair because of the wind.
Je suis surpris(e) que le coiffeur ne vende pas de peignes (m.).
I am surprised that the hairdresser doesn't sell combs.
Je suis content(e) que vous me parliez en français.
I am pleased that you are talking to me in French.

It is important to note that when the subject of the dependent verb is the same as that of the main verb, the construction with an infinitive is used. Compare:

Je voudrais partir. I'd like to leave.
Nous voudrions partir. We'd like to leave.
But
Nous voudrions que vous partiez. We'd like you to leave.

There are some irregular subjunctives, and the most important are:

être (to be)	**que je sois, il soit, nous soyons, ils soient**
avoir (to have)	**que j'aie, il ait, nous ayons, ils aient**
aller (to go)	**que j'aille, il aille, nous allions, ils aillent**
faire (to do, make)	**que je fasse, il fasse, nous fassions, ils fassent**
pouvoir (to be able)	**que je puisse, il puisse, nous puissions, ils puissent**
prendre (to take)	**que je prenne, il prenne, nous prenions, ils prennent**
savoir (to know)	**que je sache, il sache, nous sachions, ils sachent**
venir (to come)	**que je vienne, il vienne, nous venions, ils viennent**

The subjunctive is also used after the following conjunctions—those marked * require **ne** before the verb:

12

quoique	although
bien que	although
pour que	in order that
afin que	in order that
de peur que*	for fear that
à condition que	on condition that
pourvu que	provided that
jusqu'à ce que	until
à moins que*	unless
avant que*	before

Examples:

Bien qu'il sache parler français, il refuse de téléphoner à Paris.
Although he can speak French, he refuses to call Paris.

Je vous ai acheté ce portable pour que vous puissiez me parler de temps en temps.
I've bought you this mobile phone so that you can speak to me from time to time.

Je veux bien vous donner ma tablette, à condition que vous écoutiez un enregistrement d'anglais chaque soir.
I'm quite willing to give you my tablet, on condition that you listen to an English recording every evening.

A moins que vous ne m'aidiez, je ne pourrai pas finir cet exercice.
Unless you help me, I won't be able to finish this exercise.

Je dois rester ici jusqu'à ce que ma femme arrive.
I must stay here until my wife arrives.

The subjunctive is also used after:

1. a superlative:
C'est la plus grande librairie que nous ayons jamais vue.
This is the biggest bookstore we have ever seen.

2. seul (only), **premier** (first), **dernier** (last):
Paul est le seul qui puisse aller à la réunion.
Paul is the only one who can go to the meeting.

12

3. an indefinite antecedent:

Je cherche un médecin qui sache parler anglais.
I'm looking for a doctor who can speak English.
(i.e. I'm not sure that one exists)
But
Je cherche le médecin qui sait parler anglais.
I'm looking for the doctor who can speak English.
(i.e. I know he exists)

4. impersonal verbs such as:

Il faut que ...	It is necessary that ...
Il vaut mieux que ...	It is better that ...
Il est important que ...	It is important that ...
Il est possible que ...	It is possible that ...
Il est inévitable que ...	It is inevitable that ...
Il est dommage que ...	It is a shame that ...

Examples:
Il est important que nous réservions les chambres à l'avance.
It is important that we reserve the rooms in advance.
Il est dommage qu'il ne vienne pas aujourd'hui.
It is too bad that he's not coming today.

5. the negative of **penser** (to think) and **croire** (to believe)—compare:
Je pense que Caroline va à la réception.
I think that Caroline is going to the reception.
Je ne pense pas que Caroline aille à la réception.
I don't think Caroline is going to the reception.

6. quoi que (whatever):
... quoi que vous fassiez ...
... whatever you do ...

7. quel que, quelle que, quels que, quelles que (whatever):
... quelle que soit la raison ...
... whatever the reason may be ...

12

The subjunctive is also used for the third-person imperative:

Qu'il prenne le parapluie. Let him take the umbrella.
Qu'elle parte. Let her leave.
Qu'ils fassent la vaisselle. Let them wash the dishes.

Note that there is also a perfect subjunctive, which is used for actions in the past. The perfect subjunctive is formed with **avoir** or **être**:

Je suis content que vous ayez retrouvé votre portefeuille.
I am pleased that you have found your wallet.
Je suis désolé qu'elle soit tombée malade.
I am sorry that she has fallen ill.

VOCABULARY 2

le lancement	launch
le vaisseau spatial	spacecraft
le discours	speech
l'espace (m.)	space
la déclaration	statement
la conquête	conquest
la mission	mission
l'apesanteur (f.)	weightlessness
l'expérience (f.)	experiment, experience
les données (f.)	data
continuer	to continue
participer	to take part
filmer	to film
enregistrer	to record
reporter	to postpone
mener	to conduct
avoir lieu	to take place
en direct	live
quand même	still, nevertheless

12

Exercise 3

Translate:

1. I suggest that the president make a statement on television.
2. We must continue our conquest of space.
3. He would like the launch of the spacecraft to take place next week.
4. I am pleased that you are taking part in this space mission.
5. It is important that the launch should be filmed live.
6. Unless you can give me all the data recorded by the computers, I cannot take a decision.
7. We are pleased that the president has decided to postpone his speech.
8. Although the astronauts are used to weightlessness, they still have a little difficulty carrying out their experiments on board the spacecraft.

VOCABULARY 3

le/la graphologue	graphologist
le mariage	wedding, marriage
le(s) renseignement(s) (m.)	information
l'échantillon (m.)	sample
la conversation téléphonique	telephone conversation
la personnalité	personality
la conclusion	conclusion
l'écriture (f.)	handwriting
l'analyse (f.)	analysis
les félicitations (f.)	congratulations
analyser	to analyze
rédiger	to write, to draft
retarder	to delay
tout à fait	quite, completely
compatible	compatible
ordinaire	ordinary
favorable	favorable
alors	so
allô	hello (on the telephone)

Une conversation téléphonique entre un graphologue et une jeune cliente.

CLIENTE **Allô. Bonjour, monsieur. C'est vous le graphologue?**

GRAPHOLOGUE **Oui, c'est moi.**

CLIENTE **Eh bien, mon fiancé vient de fixer la date de notre mariage et …**

GRAPHOLOGUE **Félicitations, mademoiselle!**

CLIENTE **Merci. Je ne crois pas que je sois tout à fait prête pour le mariage, alors je voudrais que vous analysiez mon écriture et aussi celle de mon fiancé pour voir si nos personnalités sont compatibles.**

GRAPHOLOGUE **Oui, c'est très facile. Il faut que vous m'envoyiez un échantillon de votre écriture et de celle de votre fiancé.**

CLIENTE **Quelle sorte d'échantillon faut-il que je vous envoie?**

GRAPHOLOGUE **Je préfère que vous écriviez une lettre tout à fait ordinaire, mais il faut qu'elle soit signée.**

CLIENTE **Je doute que mon fiancé soit prêt à rédiger une lettre et à la signer sans savoir pourquoi.**

GRAPHOLOGUE **Mais il est très important qu'il n'en connaisse pas la raison.**

CLIENTE **Bon, très bien. Pour que vous puissiez arriver à une conclusion plus rapidement, est-ce qu'il faut que nous vous donnions des renseignements supplémentaires?**

GRAPHOLOGUE **Non, pas du tout.**

CLIENTE **Vous savez, cette analyse est très importante pour moi. A moins que votre rapport ne soit favorable, il est possible que je retarde le mariage.**

12

A telephone conversation between a graphologist and a young client.

CLIENT Hello. Good morning. Are you the graphologist?

GRAPHOLOGIST Yes, I am.

CLIENT Well, my fiancé has just fixed the date of our wedding and ...

GRAPHOLOGIST Congratulations!

CLIENT Thank you. I don't think I'm quite ready for marriage, so I'd like you to analyze my handwriting, and also my fiancé's, in order to see if our personalities are compatible.

GRAPHOLOGIST Yes, that's very easy. You must send me a sample of your handwriting and your fiancé's.

CLIENT What sort of sample do I have to send?

GRAPHOLOGIST I prefer you to write a perfectly ordinary letter, but it must be signed.

CLIENT I doubt whether my fiancé will be willing to write a letter and to sign it without knowing why.

GRAPHOLOGIST But it's very important that he doesn't know the reason for it.

CLIENT Okay, fine. So that you can come to a conclusion more rapidly, do we have to give you any additional information?

GRAPHOLOGIST No, not at all.

CLIENT You know, this analysis is very important for me. Unless your report is favorable, it's possible I may delay the wedding.

12

The following four exercises are not an essential part of the course, but they will certainly help you consolidate your knowledge of French if you make the effort to do them. Before you try these exercises, complete Self-assessment test 3 first.

Exercise 4

Translate back into French all the English translations of the CONVERSATIONS that have appeared in this course.

Exercise 5

Translate back into French all the English translations of the EXAMPLES that have appeared in this course.

Exercise 6

Translate back into French all the English translations of the VOCABULARY LISTS that have appeared in this course.

Exercise 7

Translate back into English all the sentences in the EXERCISE KEY.

Self-assessment test 3 A–C

This self-assessment test, based on weeks 9–12, will enable you to check your progress and to see whether any review is needed. Deduct one point for every grammatical mistake or wrong spelling. The answers and score assessment are in the key.

A. Reflexive verbs   Total: 11 points

Give the French for these sentences describing daily routines and what happened yesterday:

1. I wake up at 8 a.m.
2. I wash.
3. I shave.
4. I go to work.
5. Monique gets up at 9 o'clock.
6. She washes.
7. She dresses quickly.
8. She goes to the office.
9. Nicole and I (f.) woke up at 10 o'clock.
10. We put on our make-up.
11. We went to the station.

B. Verbs preceded by prepositions   Total: 4 points

Complete the following:

1. Il est parti [without saying] un mot.
2. Elle a hésité [before replying].
3. J'ai commencé [by criticizing] l'interprète.
4. [After having bought] un ordinateur, il a travaillé plus vite.

C. Conjunctions   Total: 5 points

Complete the following sentences with the most suitable conjunction:

1. Nous avons acheté une tente, … nous voulons faire du camping.
2. Mon père n'aime pas l'Italie, … nous sommes allés en Allemagne.
3. … tu vas chercher de la bière, je vais regarder la télévision.
4. C'est un bon camping, … où sont les toilettes?
5. … vous serez prêts, je préparerai à manger.

12

D. Numbers   Total: 12 points

Complete the following, writing the totals in words:

A. 320 + 120   **D.** 260 + 50

B. 150 + 150   **E.** 1,000 + 330

C. 580 + 200   **F.** 450 + 50

E. Peculiarities of French construction   Total: 10 points

Give the French for:

1. How long have you been in England? (Use "tu")
2. I've been working here since the 2nd of May.
3. We've been learning French for three months.
4. We've just bought an apartment.
5. They've just called a doctor.

F. Translation of "to" before an infinitive   Total: 6 points

Complete the following:

1. [We hope to] aller à la plage.
2. [They've decided to] louer une voiture.
3. [They (f.) are pleased to] voir le soleil.
4. [She intends to] acheter des lunettes de soleil.
5. [I hesitate to] faire du ski nautique.
6. [Will you (tu) have the opportunity to] faire de la planche à voile?

G. The verb **faire**   Total: 4 points

Rewrite the following using faire:

1. Quelle est votre profession?
2. Ma mère prépare un gâteau.
3. Je vais parler de la conquête de l'espace devant 100 personnes.
4. Il s'est promené au parc.

12

Self-assessment test 3 H–J

H. The imperative (with pronouns)   Total: 16 points
Make up your mind! Give the French for:

1. (the letter) Photocopy it—no, don't photocopy it.
2. (the samples) Send them—no, don't send them.
3. (the catalog) Give it to me—no, don't give it to me.
4. Telephone them—no, don't telephone them.

I. The subjunctive   Total: 8 points
Complete the following:

1. Je voudrais que [you make] un rendez-vous.
2. Je veux bien vous aider, à condition que [you finish] le travail aujourd'hui.
3. Il est dommage que [Sophie isn't coming] à la réception.
4. Nous sommes contents que [they've found] une petite maison.

J. Conversation (role-play)   Total: 24 points
Take the part of Faustine:

AHMED Est-ce que tu écoutes toujours les enregistrements que tu as achetés récemment?

FAUSTINE Yes, of course. I bought them because I have to learn English in three months.

AHMED Est-ce que tu as le temps d'écouter ces enregistrements?

FAUSTINE Yes, if I listen to them in the morning when I'm washing. My husband listens to them as well, when he's shaving. If I succeed in learning English, it'll be possible for me to get a promotion and leave for the United States.

12

Reading practice

Voyage en Europe

Quand j'ai reçu une invitation pour un mariage à Vérone, en Italie, j'étais vraiment très content. J'allais pouvoir prendre le train et voyager en Europe ! Un matin de juillet, je suis donc parti avec un sac à dos, un pass ferroviaire et un portefeuille plein d'euros. Mon aventure pouvait commencer !

J'ai pris le train de Londres à Amsterdam et j'ai passé un week-end agréable à faire du vélo le long des canaux et à goûter à des fromages hollandais délicieux. Ensuite, je suis allé à Munich et j'ai exploré le Englischer Garten, l'immense parc du centre-ville. Puis j'ai traversé les Alpes jusqu'à Lyon et j'ai poursuivi mon voyage jusque sur la côte ouest française. Cela a pris plusieurs jours, mais les paysages étaient tellement spectaculaires que cela ne m'a pas dérangé. Après m'être arrêté à Bordeaux pour y déguster son célèbre vin, j'ai passé la frontière pour me rendre en Espagne et j'ai parcouru la côte nord. J'ai fait une halte pour goûter aux pintxos à Saint Sébastien et visiter la cathédrale de Saint-Jacques-de-Compostelle. J'ai exploré le vieux Lisbonne en tramway, c'est charmant ! J'ai visité le musée du Prado à Madrid et découvert l'architecture remarquable de Gaudí à Barcelone. De là, je suis repassé en France et j'ai passé quelques jours dans les stations balnéaires chics de la Côte d'Azur.

Après avoir traversé la frontière italienne et être arrivé à Gênes, je savais que ce voyage exceptionnel touchait à sa fin. Il me restait cependant un endroit à visiter : la ville historique et romantique de Vérone. Le mariage était fantastique et j'ai mangé un des meilleurs repas de ma vie. C'était une façon parfaite de terminer un voyage inoubliable.

VOCABULARY

un mariage	wedding	**exploré**	explored
partir	set off	**immense**	huge
un sac à dos	backpack	**les paysages**	scenery
un pass		**spectaculaires**	spectacular
ferroviaire	rail pass	**cela ne m'a**	
agréable	enjoyable	**pas dérangé**	didn't mind
les canaux	canals	**charmant**	charming
délicieux	delicious	**découvert**	discovered

A tour of Europe

When I received an invitation to a wedding in Verona, Italy, I was really excited. I could take the train and go on a tour of Europe! So one morning in July, I set off with a backpack, a rail pass, and a wallet full of euros and began my adventure!

I took a train from London to Amsterdam and spent an enjoyable weekend cycling along the canals and trying delicious Dutch cheeses. Then I went to Munich and explored its huge central park, the Englischer Garten. Next, I traveled through the Alps to Lyon and then to the west coast of France. It took several days, but the scenery was so spectacular that I didn't mind. After stopping in Bordeaux to enjoy its famous wine, I crossed the border into Spain and traveled along the north coast, stopping to try pinxos in San Sebastián and visit the cathedral in Santiago de Compostela. I explored Lisbon's charming old town by trolley, visited the Prado museum in Madrid, and discovered the extraordinary architecture of Gaudí in Barcelona. From there, I returned to France and spent a few days in the stylish seaside resorts of the Côte d'Azur.

When I crossed the Italian border and arrived in Genoa, I knew my amazing tour was almost over. But I had one place left to visit: the historic and romantic city of Verona. The wedding was incredible, and I had one of the best meals of my life. It was the perfect end to an unforgettable trip.

remarquable	extraordinary
l'architecture	architecture
chic	stylish
les stations balnéaires	seaside resorts
fantastique	incredible
inoubliable	unforgettable

Key to exercises

Exercise 1: 1 le passeport. 2 l'hôtel. 3 la valise. 4 une station. 5 une leçon. 6 un livre. 7 une personne. 8 les journalistes. 9 les prix. 10 de la bière. 11 du vin. 12 des lettres. 13 des journaux. 14 des autobus.

Exercise 2: 1 Oui, elle a un journal. 2 Oui, ils ont une voiture. 3 Oui, j'ai une radio. 4 Oui, j'ai une carte. 5 Oui, nous avons une clé. 6 Oui, vous avez une tablette.

Exercise 3: 1 Non, je n'ai pas de valise. 2 Non, je n'ai pas de passeport. 3 Non, nous n'avons pas de vin. 4 Non, nous n'avons pas de livre. 5 Non, il n'a pas de tablettes. 6 Non, elle n'a pas de radio. 7 Non, vous n'avez pas de journaux. 8 Non, elles n'ont pas d'appareil-photo.

Exercise 4: 1 J'ai une voiture. 2 Je n'ai pas de clés. 3 Nous avons une valise. 4 Elle a de l'alcool. 5 Il n'a pas de journal. 6 Ils ont des livres. 7 Elles n'ont pas de cartes. 8 Vous n'avez pas d'imprimante. 9 Vous avez un appareil-photo? 10 Vous avez des tablettes? 11 Vous avez des livres? 12 Vous avez une radio?

Week 2

Exercise 1: 1 Je suis médecin. 2 Il est pilote. 3 Elle est journaliste. 4 Nous sommes banquiers. 5 Vous êtes avocat. 6 Elles sont professeur(e)s. 7 Ils sont astronautes.

Exercise 2: 1 Le banquier est pauvre. 2 La secrétaire est stupide. 3 Les médecins sont malheureux. 4 Les journaux sont ennuyeux. 5 Le vin est mauvais. 6 Le livre est difficile. 7 L'avocate est impolie. 8 La bière est bonne.

Exercise 3: 1 Nous habitons à Versailles. 2 Elle travaille à Nice. 3 Il voyage. 4 Je parle deux langues. 5 Elles pratiquent un sport. 6 Ils regardent la télévision. 7 Vous écoutez la radio. 8 Nous préparons une enquête.

Exercise 4: 1 Est-ce que tu téléphones à l'hôtel? 2 Est-ce que tu réserves une chambre? 3 Est-ce que tu invites le directeur à dîner? 4 Elle est intelligente? 5 Elle est intéressante? 6 Elle est grande? 7 Exporte-t-il des ordinateurs en France? 8 Importe-t-il des voitures? 9 Vote-t-il pour le président?

Exercise 5: a) neuf. b) deux. c) douze. d) cinq. e) quinze. f) douze. g) quatorze. h) trois.

Week 3

Exercise 1: 1 Je finis le rapport. 2 Nous garantissons l'ordinateur portable. 3 Elle choisit un gâteau. 4 Il grossit. 5 Elles maigrissent. 6 Ils remplissent les verres. 7 Nous saisissons l'occasion.

Exercise 2: 1 Ce train est rapide. 2 Cette gare est impor-tante. 3 Ce guichet est fermé. 4 Cette voiture est chère. 5 Cet ascenseur est plein. 6 Ces places sont réservées. 7 Ces compartiments sont occupés. 8 Ces billets sont valables.

Exercise 3: 1 Il a tort. 2 Elle a froid. 3 Ils ont raison. 4 Elles ont chaud.

Exercise 4: 1 Non, je ne travaille pas. 2 Non, je n'écoute pas. 3 Non, je n'ai pas faim. 4 Non, je ne choisis jamais de fromage. 5 Non, je ne téléphone jamais. 6 Non, je n'ai jamais froid. 7 Non, il ne mange rien. 8 Non, elle ne prépare rien. 9 Non, il n'exporte rien. 10 Non, nous n'invitons personne. 11 Non, nous ne choisissons personne. 12 Non, nous ne rencontrons personne. 13 Non, ils n'ont plus de voiture. 14 Non, elles n'habitent plus à Paris. 15 Non, elles ne travaillent plus.

Exercise 5: 1 Où travaillez-vous? 2 Quand regardez-vous le film? 3 Comment allez-vous? 4 Qui téléphone? 5 Qui cherchent-ils? 6 Pourquoi mangez-vous? 7 Quelles langues parlez-vous? 8 Combien de livres avez-vous? 9 Combien coûte ce journal? 10 Qu'est-ce que vous exportez?

Exercise 6: 1 Réserve deux chambres. 2 Cherche François. 3 Saisis cette occasion. 4 Choisis la méthode Hugo. 5 Monte les bagages. 6 N'en achète pas trop. 7 Ne finis pas la glace. 8 Ne fume pas. 9 Parlons français. 10 Écoutons la radio. 11 Finissons le rapport.

Week 4

Exercise 1: 1 J'ai habité en France. 2 J'ai travaillé en Italie. 3 J'ai réservé les chambres. 4 Elle a écouté la radio. 5 Elle a regardé la télévision. 6 Elle a préparé le rapport. 7 Il a grossi. 8 Il a choisi le fromage. 9 Il a fini le livre. 10 Nous avons copié le document. 11 Nous avons acheté la voiture. 12 Nous avons téléphoné. 13 Vous avez garanti l'ordinateur portable. 14 Vous avez saisi l'occasion. 15 Vous avez invité le président. 16 Ils ont maigri. 17 Elles ont dépensé 15 euros. 18 Elles ont traversé la Manche.

Exercise 2: 1 Non, je n'ai pas réservé la chambre. 2 Non, je n'ai pas écouté la radio. 3 Non, il n'a pas regardé le film. 4 Non, elle n'a pas préparé le document. 5 Non, nous n'avons pas fini. 6 Non, ils n'ont pas choisi. 7 Non, elles n'ont pas mangé.

Exercise 3: 1 Votre premier vol. 2 Attachez votre ceinture de sécurité. 3 Où sont nos billets? 4 Voici son passeport. 5 Voici sa place. 6 Leurs valises sont dans l'avion. 7 Où sont mes journaux?

Exercise 4: 1 C'est ennuyeux. 2 C'est mauvais. 3 C'est impossible. 4 C'est difficile. 5 C'est affreux. 6 C'est tôt.

Exercise 5: 1 Il est deux heures et quart. 2 Il est quatre heures et demie. 3 Il est six heures. 4 Il est huit heures vingt. 5 Le train arrive à dix heures et quart. 6 Le car arrive à midi moins le quart (or minuit moins le quart). 7 Le bateau part à midi vingt-cinq. 8 L'avion part à une heure moins le quart. 9 La présidente arrive à neuf heures et quart. 10 La conférence de presse est à dix heures et quart.

Exercise 6: 1 Le premier janvier. 2 Le premier mai. 3 Le quatorze juillet. 4 Le vingt-cinq décembre. 5 Le onze novembre. 6 Le vingt et un mars.

Exercise 7: 1 J'ai travaillé lundi. 2 J'ai écouté la radio mardi. 3 J'ai regardé la télévision mercredi. 4 J'ai fini le rapport jeudi. 5 J'ai acheté un livre vendredi. 6 J'ai téléphoné à ma femme samedi. 7 J'ai parlé espagnol dimanche. 8 Je travaille le lundi. 9 Elle écoute la radio le mardi. 10 Nous regardons la télévision le mercredi.

Self-assessment test 1

A: 1 le médecin. 2 l'ordinateur. 3 du vin. 4 de la bière. 5 ma voiture. 6 mes clés. 7 ce train. 8 ces journaux.

B: 1 riche. 2 heureux. 3 ennuyeux. 4 affreux. 5 difficile.

C: 1 regarder. 2 écouter. 3 choisir. 4 pratiquer.
5 attacher. 6 réserver. 7 voyager. 8 saisir.
9 consulter. 10 traverser.

D: 1 six heures et quart. 2 neuf heures moins le
quart. 3 dix heures vingt. 4 midi/minuit moins
le quart.

E: 1 mercredi. 2 dimanche. 3 vendredi. 4 mardi.

F: Jeudi means 'on Thursday'; le jeudi means 'on
Thursdays', 'every Thursday'.

G: 1 le deux février. 2 le cinq avril. 3 le douze juin.
4 le trente et un août.

H: 1 Non, j'ai réservé les chambres lundi. 2 Non, il a
fini le livre lundi. 3 Non, elle a photocopié le
document lundi. 4 Non, ils ont téléphoné lundi.

I: 1 Je n'ai pas fini le rapport. 2 Elle n'a pas
téléphoné à son mari samedi. 3 Nous n'avons pas
visité l'Italie. 4 Ils n'ont pas maigri.

J: a) vingt-neuf. b) trente-six. c) quarante-cinq.
d) trente et un. e) quarante-quatre. f) cinquante.
g) quinze. h) soixante-deux. i) seize.

K: avoir

L: Nous désirons passer deux semaines en France au
printemps. Nous avons visité l'Italie en août, mais
nous avons trouvé la chaleur insupportable.
• Non, par le train, c'est plus agréable. • Oui,
d'accord. Départ le neuf avril, retour le vingt-trois
avril.

Score:

80–100%	=	Excellent!
60–79%	=	Good! You're progressing well!
45–59%	=	Satisfactory, but a review would be useful.
Below 45%	=	You might want to review the previous weeks before moving on.

Week 5

Exercise 1: 1 Je vends ma voiture. 2 Il attend sa femme. 3 Nous rendons soixante euros. 4 Cela dépend de mes parents. 5 Est-ce qu'elles entendent la musique? 6 Elle a vendu sa maison. 7 Nous n'avons pas répondu. 8 Avez-vous descendu les bagages? 9 Attends-tu ton frère? 10 As-tu perdu ta mère?

Exercise 2: 1 Est-ce que vous avez pris le train? 2 J'ai appris le français. 3 Apprenez-vous la langue? 4 Comprenez-vous? 5 Tu as souvent surpris ton professeur?

Exercise 3: 1 J'ai mis une annonce dans le journal. 2 Il a permis à son employé de partir tôt. 3 Vous avez promis de répondre à la lettre? 4 Elle a soumis le rapport ce matin. 5 Mettez-vous le livre dans la valise? 6 Permettent-ils à leurs enfants de rentrer tard? 7 Nous promettons de parler français. 8 Soumettez-vous déjà le projet?

Exercise 4: 1 rapidement. 2 facilement. 3 finalement. 4 heureusement. 5 attentivement. 6 lentement. 7 complètement. 8 normalement. 9 principalement. 10 temporairement.

Exercise 5: 1 Le rapport? Il est très important. 2 La bière? Elle est mauvaise. 3 La poche? Elle est pleine. 4 L'appareil? Il est excellent. 5 Le restaurant? Il est fermé. 6 La qualité? Elle est très bonne. 7 Les produits? Ils sont français. 8 Les messages? Ils sont en anglais. 9 L'explication? Elle n'est pas claire. 10 Le portable? Il n'est pas cher.

Exercise 6: 1 Oui, elle vous cherche. 2 Oui, elle me consulte. 3 Oui, je le rencontre. 4 Oui, je la photocopie. 5 Oui, il l'invite. 6 Oui, il les exporte. 7 Oui, nous le comprenons. 8 Oui, nous la branchons. 9 Oui, nous le mettons en marche. 10 Oui, nous le photocopions. 11 Oui, elles nous répondent en français. 12 Oui, ils lui téléphonent. 13 Oui, ils lui téléphonent. 14 Oui, ils leur téléphonent. 15 Oui, je lui parle. 16 Oui, je leur réponds. 17 Oui, je leur permets de rentrer tard.

Exercise 7: 1 Oui, je l'ai invité. 2 Oui, je l'ai invitée. 3 Oui, je les ai invités. 4 Oui, il les a exportées. 5 Oui, elle l'a consulté. 6 Oui, elle l'a consultée. 7 Oui, elle les a consultés. 8 Oui, ils l'ont branchée. 9 Oui, ils les ont réservées. 10 Oui, ils l'ont perdue. 11 Oui, nous l'avons compris. 12 Oui, nous l'avons comprise. 13 Oui, nous les avons comprises. 14 Oui, nous les avons compris. 15 Oui, je l'ai mise dans ma poche.

Week 6

Exercise 1: 1 Il y a une serviette sur la table. 2 Il y a un taxi devant l'hôtel. 3 Il y a un restaurant derrière l'église. 4 Il y a un supermarché à côté de la banque. 5 Il y a une librairie en face de l'université. 6 Est-ce qu'il y a une boulangerie près de la gare? 7 Est-ce qu'il y a des livres anglais à la bibliothèque? 8 Est-ce qu'il y a un tunnel sous la Manche? 9 Je vais au cinéma. 10 Elle va aux États-Unis. 11 Avez-vous le numéro de téléphone du théâtre? 12 J'ai acheté un journal pour mon ami(e). 13 Elle apprend le français avec des amis. 14 C'est difficile de travailler sans mon portable. 15 Mangeons après le spectacle. 16 Téléphonons avant 9 heures.

Exercise 2: 1 Le banquier est plus riche que le professeur. 2 Le facteur est plus pauvre que l'avocate. 3 Le pilote est aussi courageux que l'astronaute. 4 Le français n'est pas aussi difficile que le russe. 5 Elle parle plus distinctement que Paul. 6 Il écoute plus attentivement que son frère.

Exercise 3: 1 Oui, c'est le restaurant le plus chic du monde. 2 Oui, c'est la plus grande librairie du monde. 3 Oui, c'est le magasin le plus célèbre du monde. 4 Oui, c'est la plus belle cathédrale du monde. 5 Oui, c'est la meilleure bière du monde. 6 Oui, c'est le parc le plus agréable du monde. 7 Oui, c'est la ville la plus intéressante du monde. 8 Oui, c'est la voiture la plus confortable du monde. 9 Oui, c'est l'avion le plus impressionnant du monde.

Exercise 4: 1 Il pleut. 2 Il y a du brouillard. 3 Il y a du vent. 4 Il fait froid. 5 Il y a du soleil. 6 Il neige. 7 Il fait chaud. 8 Il fait mauvais. 9 Il fait beau.

Exercise 5: A. 1 Je suis médecin. 2 Ce matin, je suis arrivé à l'hôpital à 7 heures. 3 Je suis allé à une réunion à 10 heures. 4 Je suis parti avec deux infirmières. B. 1 Je suis journaliste. 2 Hier, je suis allée à une conférence de presse. 3 Je suis montée au restaurant à une heure. 4 Je suis retournée au bureau très tard. C. 1 Nicole et Sophie sont étudiantes. 2 Ce matin, elles sont allées à l'université à 9 heures. 3 Elles sont restées toute la journée à la bibliothèque. 4 Elles sont revenues à la maison à 5 heures.

Exercise 6: 1 Les ingénieurs sont arrivés hier. 2 Les infirmiers sont déjà partis. 3 Nous sommes revenues tôt. 4 Tu es descendu. 5 Est-ce que la docteure est restée toute la journée? 6 Êtes-vous revenu très tard?

Exercise 7: 1 Je voudrais une carte postale. 2 Je voudrais un timbre. 3 Je voudrais un plan de la ville. 4 Je voudrais un journal américain. 5 Je voudrais du lait. 6 Je voudrais du sucre. 7 Je voudrais du thé. 8 Je voudrais téléphoner à New York. 9 Je voudrais régler la note.

Exercise 8: 1 Il me faut un crayon. 2 Il me faut un stylo. 3 Il lui faut une gomme. 4 Il lui faut du papier. 5 Il leur faut des enveloppes. 6 Il leur faut des timbres. 7 Il leur faut des allumettes.

Week 7

Exercise 1: 1 Non, j'ai beaucoup de cravates. 2 Non, j'ai beaucoup de costumes. 3 Non, j'ai beaucoup de robes. 4 Oui, il a maintenant trop de pantalons. 5 Oui, elle a maintenant trop de jupes. 6 Oui, elle a maintenant trop de foulards. 7 Il a peu de patience. 8 Avez-vous (or as-tu) mis assez de chemises dans la valise? 9 J'ai plus de gilets que Manon. 10 Vous avez moins de costumes que Pierre.

Exercise 2: 1 Je vais écouter la radio. 2 Je vais acheter un journal. 3 Je vais étudier le français. 4 Je vais faire les courses. 5 Il réparera la voiture. 6 Il jouera au tennis. 7 Il écrira une lettre. 8 Il visitera le musée. 9 Ils rangeront l'appartement. 10 Ils organiseront une réunion. 11 Ils iront à une conférence internationale. 12 Ils passeront un week-end à Londres. 13 Elle finira sa lettre. 14 Nous irons au théâtre la semaine prochaine. 15 Vous surprendrez votre père. 16 Tu choisiras ta robe le mois prochain.

Exercise 3: 1 Je peux acheter les légumes au marché. 2 Je peux préparer le rapport. 3 Nous ne pouvons pas arriver lundi. 4 Nous ne pouvons pas lire son écriture. 5 Elle doit signer le contrat. 6 Elle doit arrêter de fumer. 7 Ils ne doivent pas décourager les étudiants. 8 Ils ne doivent pas garer la voiture devant l'hôpital. 9 Il veut faire le tour du monde. 10 Il veut dépenser moins d'argent. 11 Est-ce que tu sais (or Sais-tu) conduire? 12 Est-ce que tu sais (or Sais-tu) nager?

Exercise 4: Check your list of countries using section 7.4 or, if you've been adventurous, a dictionary!

Exercise 5: 1 Nous passons nos vacances en Grèce. 2 As-tu l'intention d'aller au Japon? 3 L'Allemagne exporte des voitures en France. 4 Est-ce que le/la diplomate est arrivé(e) en Russie?

Exercise 6: a) Vingt. b) Vingt-deux. c) Trente et un. d) Quarante-sept. e) Cinquante-neuf. f) Soixante et un. g) Soixante-dix. h) Soixante-dix-neuf. i) Quatre-vingt-un. j) Quatre-vingt-onze. k) Quatre-vingt-dix-neuf. l) Cent.

Week 8

Exercise 1: 1 Il jouait au football. 2 Il allait à la pêche. 3 Il collectionnait des timbres. 4 Elle chantait. 5 Elle écoutait des disques. 6 Nous apprenions l'espagnol. 7 Nous habitions dans une petite maison. 8 Nous faisions de la photo (graphie). 9 Je finissais la traduction quand j'ai entendu un bruit en haut. 10 Elle faisait les courses quand elle a perdu son porte-monnaie. 11 Ils regardaient la télévision quand le cambrioleur est entré dans la maison.

Exercise 2: 1 L'hôtel que vous cherchez est à droite.
2 Je voudrais la chambre qui donne sur le parc.
3 La chambre, que nous avons réservée pour vous, est à côté de l'ascenseur. 4 J'ai apporté le petit déjeuner que votre mari a commandé. 5 Où est la télévision qui ne marche pas? 6 Les valises, qui sont dans le hall, sont très lourdes. 7 La réceptionniste à qui vous avez parlé est bilingue. 8 Le client, dont le fils est malade, est dans la chambre 5. 9 N'avez-vous pas compris ce que la femme de ménage vous a dit?
10 La note que vous avez préparée est correcte.

Exercise 3: 1 Si j'étais riche, je ferais le tour du monde. 2 Si je ne travaillais pas, je peindrais et je dessinerais. 3 S'il avait beaucoup de temps, il apprendrait le portugais. 4 Si elle parlait français, elle travaillerait comme interprète. 5 Si elle parlait allemand, elle travaillerait comme professeure bilingue. 6 Si vous étiez marié, vous achèteriez une maison. 7 S'ils étaient au chômage, ils chercheraient du travail. 8 Si elles avaient des enfants, elles iraient au parc. 9 Si j'avais le temps, je lirais beaucoup.
10 Si nous voulions maigrir, nous mangerions moins et ferions du sport.

Exercise 4: 1 … avec lui. 2 … à côté d'elle. 3 … sans eux. 4 … qu'elles. 5 … que lui. 6 … Elle. 7 Ce sont (or C'est) eux qui …

Exercise 5: 1 Je ne sais pas si Jules a fini son travail.
2 Je ne connais pas les Dupont. 3 Savez-vous où je peux louer un ordinateur? 4 Savez-vous si le médecin est libre? 5 Est-ce que Nabila connaît ma tante?

Exercise 6: 1 Je ne vous dérange pas. Je pensais justement à vous. Vous n'êtes pas trop occupée? … quand vous avez frappé à la porte. À qui est-ce que vous écriviez? À propos, comment va votre travail? Qu'est-ce que vous feriez de tout ce temps libre? Vous feriez mieux de prendre votre retraite tout de suite.

Self-assessment test 2

A: 1 devant. 2 à côté de. 3 en face de. 4 sous. 5 près de. 6 sans. 7 après. 8 avant.

B: 1 Je suis journaliste. 2 Ce matin, je suis arrivé(e) à l'hôtel à sept heures. 3 Je suis allé(e) à une conférence internationale à dix heures. 4 Je suis parti(e) très tard.

C: 1 Il pleut. 2 Il fait chaud. / Il y a du soleil. 3 Il y a du brouillard. 4 Il fait froid. / Il neige. 5 Il fait froid. / Il y a du vent.

D: 1 le Portugal. 2 le Japon. 3 les États-Unis. 4 la Grèce. 5 l'Espagne. 6 l'Italie. 7 les Pays-Bas. 8 la Chine. 9 la Belgique. 10 la France. 11 l'Angleterre. 12 le Danemark.

E: a) cinquante-huit. b) soixante-dix. c) soixante-quinze. d) quatre-vingt-trois. e) quatre-vingt-dix. f) quatre-vingt-dix-neuf. g) cent.

F: 1 Il jouait au football. 2 Elle apprenait l'anglais.

3 Ils habitaient dans une grande maison. 4 Ils faisaient les courses quand elle a perdu son porte-monnaie.

G: 1 Si j'étais riche, je visiterais le Japon et la Chine. 2 Si elle parlait italien, elle travaillerait comme interprète. 3 Si tu étais au chômage, tu chercherais du travail. 4 Si nous avions beaucoup de temps, nous lirions beaucoup.

H: a) Savoir means 'to know a fact'. Connaître is used with the meaning of 'to be acquainted with' (people, places, etc.). b) Je ne sais pas jouer ... means 'I do not know how to ...'; je ne peux pas jouer ... means something (such as a broken finger) prevents me from playing.

I: • J'ai décidé de changer de vie. Je vais regarder la télévision moins souvent. Je mangerai plus de fruits. Je ferai du sport chaque matin. Je dépenserai moins d'argent en vêtements. • Oui, j'aurai plus de temps et plus d'argent, et je serai en meilleure santé.

Score

80–100%	=	Excellent. You're doing really well!
60–79%	=	Very good.
45–59%	=	Satisfactory, but try to find time to study a little every day.
Below 45%	=	It would be a good idea to review so you can consolidate your knowledge before going on.

Week 9

Exercise 1: 1 Mon rhume est pire que celui de ma sœur. 2 Cet hôpital est plus moderne que celui que la Princesse a visité l'année dernière. 3 Quel chirurgien a effectué la greffe du cœur? Celui-ci ou celui-là? 4 Avez-vous rendez-vous (or un rendez-vous) avec ce dentiste-ci ou celui-là? 5 Le/la kinésithérapeute m'a donné ceci. 6 Le/la pharmacien(ne) a préparé cela. 7 C'est votre nouvelle ordonnance. 8 Ce sont vos patients.

Exercise 2: 1 Le barman t'a servi ton whisky, mais où est le mien? 2 Mon poisson est délicieux; le tien n'est pas frais. 3 J'ai payé notre addition et ils ont payé la leur. 4 Est-ce que ce chapeau est à toi ou à ton ami? 5 Avec quoi veux-tu manger ce plat chinois? Avec un couteau et une fourchette? Quoi? Non! Avec des baguettes. 6 Quel est le numéro de téléphone du restaurant italien? 7 Quels légumes a-t-elle commandés? 8 Qu'est-ce qui sent si bon? 9 Voici une liste des meilleurs restaurants de Paris; lequel préfères-tu? 10 A qui est cette cuillère?

Exercise 3: 1 Ils chantent mal. 2 Ne parlez pas si bas. 3 Il va souvent chez ses parents. 4 Nous avons déjà mangé. 5 Il va sûrement pleuvoir ou neiger. 6 Elle prend un bain en bas. 7 Elles ont fait les courses hier.

Week 10

Exercise 1: 1 Il se réveille à 7 heures du matin.
2 Il se lave. 3 Il se rase. 4 Il va au travail. 5 Elle se lève à 8 heures du matin. 6 Elle prend une douche. 7 Elle se coiffe. 8 Elle se maquille. 9 Elle va à la gare. 10 Nous nous lavons. 11 Nous nous habillons vite. 12 Nous nous promenons. 13 Nous nous couchons à dix heures du soir. 14 Je me suis amusée. 15 Vous ne vous êtes pas trompée. 16 Elles se reposent. 17 Ils ont lavé la voiture eux-mêmes.
18 Nous nous brossons les dents chaque matin.

Exercise 2: 1 Il a quitté la maison sans dire un mot.
2 Elle est habituée à écouter la radio dans sa chambre. 3 Avant de réparer la lampe, il a téléphoné à l'électricien(ne). 4 Après avoir préparé le petit déjeuner, il a fait le ménage. 5 Ma mère a commencé par dire que toute la famille était en bonne santé et a fini par souhaiter à tout le monde une bonne année. 6 Ces enregistrements sont excellents pour apprendre le français.

Exercise 3: 1 J'ai l'intention d'acheter des lunettes de soleil. 2 Sera-t-il possible de faire des excursions?
3 Nous préférons louer un appartement. 4 Ils m'ont invitée à aller à la pêche. 5 J'hésite à faire du ski nautique. 6 Aurez-vous l'occasion de faire de la planche à voile?

Exercise 4: 1 Est-ce-que vous me l'avez donné?
2 Il nous les a promises. 3 Il a l'intention de me les vendre. 4 Je le lui ai envoyé. 5 Il la lui montre.
6 Nous les leur avons données.

Exercise 1: 1 Puisque (or Comme) l'ami de Paul vient camper avec nous, nous devrons acheter un sac de couchage supplémentaire. 2 Quand vous saurez parler français, nous irons faire du camping en France. 3 Saisissez-vous chaque occasion pour parler français, quand vous êtes en Belgique? 4 Je n'aime pas ce camping parce qu'il n'y a pas de piscine. 5 Nous sommes quatre mais nous avons seulement (or nous n'avons que) trois sacs de couchage. 6 La voiture est tombée en panne, donc nous avons décidé de camper dans un champ.

Exercise 2: a) deux cent cinquante. b) trois cents. c) quatre cent trente. d) cinq cent soixante-dix. e) six cent quatre-vingts. f) mille quatre cent quarante.

Exercise 3: 1 la première fête. 2 le deuxième (second) spectacle. 3 la troisième boîte de nuit. 4 le quatrième théâtre. 5 le cinquième concert. 6 le sixième opéra. 7 le septième cinéma. 8 la huitième patinoire. 9 le neuvième ballet. 10 le dixième restaurant.

Exercise 4: 1 L'importance de la décision a été soulignée par le président de la République française. 2 La Grande-Bretagne sera reliée au continent par un tunnel ferroviaire en 1993. 3 Un lien routier sera construit plus tard. 4 Cette décision historique a été annoncée à Lille. 5 Les touristes étrangers ont souvent été découragés par la traversée de la Manche.

Exercise 5: 1 Elle s'est cassé le bras en faisant du ski. 2 Je suis tombé en faisant du roller. 3 En allant aux cours du soir trois fois par semaine, il a obtenu son diplôme. 4 Voyant que le conducteur était blessé, le policier a appelé les secours. 5 En téléphonant, vous aurez la réponse tout de suite.

Exercise 6: 1 Téléphonez-lui – non, ne lui téléphonez pas. 2 Envoyez-leur cette brochure – non, ne la leur envoyez pas. 3 Photocopiez ce document – non, ne le photocopiez pas. 4 Donnez-moi le catalogue – non, ne me le donnez pas. 5 Envoyez-lui les échantillons – non, ne les lui envoyez pas. 6 Soyez ici à 9 heures – non, à 8 heures. 7 Voulez-vous bien faire des heures supplémentaires?

Exercise 7: 1 Je suis marié(e) depuis cinq ans. 2 J'habite dans cette maison depuis quatre ans. 3 Je travaille pour cette banque depuis trois ans. 4 J'ai cette voiture depuis deux ans. 5 J'apprends à jouer du piano depuis un an.

Exercise 8: 1 Mais je viens d'appeler un docteur. 2 Mais je viens de prévenir les pompiers. 3 Mais je viens de vous montrer mon permis de conduire. 4 Mais les ambulances viennent de transporter les blessés à l'hôpital. 5 Mais je viens de vous donner mon adresse.

Week 12

Exercise 1: 1 Qu'est-ce que vous faites dans la vie?
2 Ma sœur fait une tarte aux pommes. 3 Je vais
faire une conférence sur la psychologie devant 200
personnes. 4 Elle a fait une promenade au parc hier.
5 Il fait de la fièvre. 6 Ne fais pas l'idiot. 7 J'ai fait
travailler mon fils. 8 Je me fais construire une
maison à Avignon.

Exercise 2: 1 he gave. 2 I sold. 3 we finished.
4 she had. 5 I was. 6 you had. 7 he took.
8 she went out. 9 they read. 10 they put.

Exercise 3: 1 Je suggère que le président fasse une
déclaration à la télévision. 2 Il faut que nous
continuions notre conquête de l'espace. 3 Il voudrait
que le lancement du vaisseau spatial ait lieu la
semaine prochaine. 4 Je suis content que vous
participiez à cette mission spatiale. 5 Il est important
que le lancement soit filmé en direct. 6 A moins que
vous ne puissiez me donner toutes les données
enregistrées par les ordinateurs, je ne peux pas
prendre de décision. 7 Nous sommes contents que le
prési-dent ait décidé de reporter son discours.
8 Bien que les astronautes soient habitués à
l'apesanteur, ils ont quand même un peu de mal à
mener leurs expériences à bord du vaisseau spatial.

Self-assessment test 3

A: 1 Je me réveille à huit heures du matin.
2 Je me lave. 3 Je me rase. 4 Je vais au travail.
5 Monique se lève à neuf heures. 6 Elle se lave.
7 Elle s'habille vite. 8 Elle va au bureau. 9 (Hier)
Nicole et moi, nous nous sommes réveillées à dix
heures. 10 Nous nous sommes maquillées.
11 Nous sommes allées à la gare.

B: 1 sans dire. 2 avant de répondre. 3 par critiquer.
4 Après avoir acheté.

C: car/parce que. 2 donc. 3 Pendant que. 4 mais.
5 Quand/ Aussitôt que.

D: a) quatre cent quarante. b) trois cents. c) sept
cent quatre-vingts. d) trois cent dix. e) mille trois
cent trente. f) cinq cents.

E: 1 Depuis quand es-tu en Angleterre? / Depuis
combien de temps es-tu en Angleterre? 2 Je travaille
ici depuis le deux mai. 3 Nous apprenons le français
depuis trois mois. 4 Nous venons d'acheter un
appartement. 5 Ils viennent d'appeler un médecin /
docteur.

F: 1 Nous espérons aller à la plage. 2 Ils ont décidé
de louer une voiture. 3 Elles sont contentes de voir
le soleil. 4 Elle a l'intention d'acheter des lunettes de
soleil. 5 J'hésite à faire du ski nautique. 6 Auras-tu
l'occasion de faire de la planche à voile?

G: 1 Qu'est-ce que vous faites dans la vie? 2 Ma mère fait un gâteau. 3 Je vais faire une conférence sur la conquête de l'espace devant cent personnes. 4 Il a fait une promenade au parc.

H: 1 Photocopiez-la – non, ne la photocopiez pas. 2 Envoyez-les – non, ne les envoyez pas. 3 Donnez-le-moi – non, ne me le donnez pas. 4 Téléphonez-leur – non, ne leur téléphonez pas.

I: 1 Je voudrais que vous fixiez un rendez-vous. 2 Je veux bien vous aider, à condition que vous finissiez le travail aujourd'hui. 3 Il est dommage que Sophie ne vienne pas à la réception. 4 Nous sommes contents qu'ils aient trouvé une petite maison.

J: • Oui, bien sûr. Je les ai achetés parce que je dois apprendre l'anglais en trois mois. • Oui, je les écoute le matin quand je me lave. Mon mari les écoute aussi, quand il se rase. Si je réussis à apprendre l'anglais, il me sera possible d'obtenir une promotion et de partir aux États-Unis.

Score:

80–100%	=	Congratulations! You've made good use of this course!
60–79%	=	Well done! With a little review, you'll be able to improve your score even more.
45–59%	=	Satisfactory. Remember that the key to success is daily study and practice.
Below 45%	=	More review is needed. Try writing out new words and expressions as you learn them, as this helps to memorize them.

Mini-dictionary

This mini-dictionary contains the most important words found in the book, plus a few others that you may find useful. See sections 4.7–4.10 for seasons, months of the year, dates, and days of the week.

able to, can pouvoir
above au-dessus de
abroad à l'étranger
across from en face (adv.), en face de (prep.)
actor acteur, actrice
address adresse (f.)
advance: in advance à l'avance
advertisement annonce (f.)
advertising publicité (f.)
advise conseiller
after après
afternoon après-midi (m. or f.)
afterward ensuite
again encore
agency agence (f.)
ago il y a
agree: I agree je suis d'accord
air-conditioning climatisation (f.)
airline company compagnie (f.) aérienne
airplane avion (m.)
alcohol alcool (m.)
all tout
allow permettre (irreg.)
already déjà
also aussi
although bien que, quoique
always toujours
ambulance ambulance (f.)
ambulance driver ambulancier (m.), -ière (f.)
America Amérique (f.)
American américain, Américain (m.), -e (f.)
analyze analyser
and et

announce annoncer
annoying énervant(e)
answer (vb.) répondre
antique dealer antiquaire (m. and f.)
apartment appartement (m.)
apple pomme (f.)
appointment rendez-vous (m.)
appreciate apprécier
approve (of) approuver
arm bras (m.)
armchair fauteuil (m.)
arrive arriver
ask (for) demander
astronaut astronaute (m and f.)
attach attacher
aunt tante
avoid éviter

bad mauvais(e)
badly mal
bag sac (m.)
  handbag sac à main
bakery boulangerie (f.)
bank banque (f.)
banker banquier (m.), -ière (f.)
bar bar (m.)
bath bain (m.)
be (to be) être (irreg.)
beach plage (f.)
beautiful beau, belle
because parce que
bed lit (m.)
  to go to bed se coucher
bedroom chambre (f.)
beer bière (f.)
before avant

begin commencer
behind derrière
Belgium Belgique (f.)
better meilleur(e), mieux
between entre
bicycle vélo (m.)
big grand(e)
bilingual bilingue
bill addition, note (f.)
black noir(e)
blood pressure tension (f.)
blue bleu(e)
boat bateau (m.)
book livre (m.)
book (vb.) réserver
bookstore librairie (f.)
boring ennuyeux, -euse
  to be bored s'ennuyer
boss patron (m.), -ne (f.)
bottle bouteille (f.)
brand marque (f.)
brave courageux, -euse
bread pain (m.)
break (vb.) casser
break down tomber en
  panne
breakdown panne (f.)
breakfast petit déjeuner (m.)
bring apporter, amener
bring down descendre
bring up monter
Britain Grande-Bretagne (f.)
British britannique
broadcast émission (f.)
brochure brochure (f.)
brother frère
brown brun(e)
build construire (irreg.)
burglar cambrioleur, -euse (f.)
burn (vb.) brûler
bus autobus (m.)
business affaires (f. pl.)
businessperson homme
  d'affaires, femme d'affaires
busy occupé(e)
but mais

butcher shop boucherie (f.)
buy acheter

cake gâteau (m.)
call (vb.) appeler
  to be called s'appeler
camera appareil-photo (m.)
camp (vb.) camper
can (to be able) pouvoir (irreg.)
Canada Canada (m.)
cancel annuler
car voiture (f.)
card carte (f.)
cash: to pay in cash payer en
  espèces
cash register caisse (f.)
castle château (m.)
cathedral cathédrale (f.)
change (vb.) changer
Channel La Manche (f.)
check chèque (m.)
check (vb.) vérifier
cheese fromage (m.)
China Chine (f.)
Chinese chinois, Chinois (m.), -e (f.)
choose choisir
church église (f.)
clean (vb.) nettoyer
cleaner homme/femme de ménage
client client (m.), -e (f.)
close (vb.) fermer
clothes vêtements (m. pl.)
coach car (m.)
coffee café (m.)
cold froid(e)
  to be cold avoir froid
  to have a cold avoir un rhume
color couleur (f.)
come venir (irreg.)
comfortable confortable
complaint plainte (f.)
computer ordinateur (m.)
  (computer) software logiciel (m.)
conference conférence (f.)
confirm confirmer
congratulate féliciter

consult consulter
continue continuer
contract contrat (m.)
copy (vb.) copier
correct (vb.) corriger
cost (vb.) coûter
country pays (m.)
create créer
credit card carte (f.) de crédit
criticize critiquer
cross (vb.) traverser
cup tasse (f.)
customs douane (f.)
cut (vb.) couper

dance (vb.) danser
dangerous dangereux, -euse
date date (f.); rendez-vous (m.)
daughter fille
decide décider
deckchair chaise (f.) longue
deep profond(e)
degree (univ.) diplôme (m.)
  (universitaire)
delicious délicieux, -euse
dentist dentiste (m. and f.)
departure départ (m.)
deposit: to leave a deposit
  verser un acompte (m.)
dial (vb.) composer
  (un numéro)
dictionary dictionnaire (m.)
diet régime (m.)
difficult difficile
dinner dîner (m.)
director directeur (m.),
  -trice (f.)
dirty sale
discourage décourager
discuss discuter de
disease maladie (f.)
disembark débarquer
dish plat (m.)
disturb déranger
dive (vb.) plonger
do faire (irreg.)

doctor médecin (m. and f.),
  docteur (m.), -e (f.)
doubt (vb.) douter
downstairs en bas
dreadful affreux, -euse
dress robe (f.)
drink (vb.) boire (irreg.)
drive (vb.) conduire (irreg.),
  rouler
driver conducteur (m.), -trice (f.)
driver's license permis (m.)
  de conduire

each chaque
early tôt
earn gagner
east est
easy facile
eat manger
efficient efficace
electrician électricien (m.),
  -ienne (f.)
elevator ascenseur (m.)
embassy ambassade (f.)
emergency: in an emergency
  en cas d'urgence
encourage encourager
end fin (f.)
engine moteur (m.)
engineer ingénieur (m.), -e (f.)
England Angleterre (f.)
English anglais(e)
enjoy oneself s'amuser
enough assez
enter entrer
entertainment divertissement (m.)
envelope enveloppe (f.)
especially surtout
euro euro (m.)
European Union Union
  européenne (f.)
even même
evening soir (m.)
everyone tout le monde
everything tout
everywhere partout

exactly exactement
excellent excellent(e)
excursion excursion (f.)
expensive cher, chère
explanation explication (f.)
export exporter
extra supplément (m.)

fall (vb.) tomber
family famille (f.)
famous célèbre
far loin
fashion mode (f.)
fast rapide
father père
fever fièvre (f.)
field champ (m.)
fill remplir
film film (m.)
find trouver
fine beau; bien
finish (vb.) finir
fire incendie (m.)
fire exit issue (f.) de secours
firefighters pompiers (m.)
first premier, première
fish poisson (m.)
fishing pêche (f.)
  to go fishing aller à la pêche
fishmonger's poissonnerie (f.)
flag drapeau (m.)
flight vol (m.)
fog brouillard (m.)
food nourriture (f.)
for pour
forbid interdire, défendre
foreign étranger, étrangère
forget oublier
forgive pardonner
fork fourchette (f.)
fortunately heureusement
free libre **(available)**,
  gratuit **(free of charge)**
French français(e)
fresh frais, fraîche
friend ami (m.), -e (f.)

from de
front: in front of devant
fruit fruit(s) (m.)
full plein(e)

garage garage (m.)
garden jardin (m.)
gasoline essence (f.)
generally généralement
German allemand(e)
Germany Allemagne (f.)
get obtenir (irreg.)
get up se lever
gift cadeau (m.)
give donner
give back rendre
glad content(e)
glass verre (m.)
glove gant (m.)
go aller (irreg.)
go down descendre
go out sortir (irreg.)
go up monter
good bon, bonne
goodbye au revoir
government gouvernement (m.)
gray gris(e)
Great Britain Grande-Bretagne (f.)
Greece Grèce (f.)
group groupe (m.)
guarantee (vb.) garantir
guide guide (m. and f.)
guide book guide (m.)

haggle marchander
hair cheveux (m. pl.)
hairdresser coiffeur (m.), -euse (f.)
half moitié (f.)
hall hall (m.)
ham jambon (m.)
hand main (f.)
handwriting écriture (f.)
happen arriver, se passer
happy heureux, -euse
harbor port (m.)
hat chapeau (m.)

hate (vb.) détester
have avoir (irreg.)
have to (must) devoir (irreg.)
hayfever rhume (m.) des foins
head tête (f.)
health santé (f.)
hear entendre
heart cœur (m.)
heavy lourd(e)
help (vb.) aider
her sa
here ici
here is voici
hers sien (m.), sienne (f.)
highway autoroute (f.)
hire louer
his son
hope (vb.) espérer
hospital hôpital (m.)
hot chaud(e)
hotel hôtel (m.)
house maison (f.)
how comment
how much, how many combien
hungry: to be hungry avoir faim
hurry se dépêcher
husband mari, époux

ice glace (f.)
ice cream glace (f.)
identification pièce (f.) d'identité
ill malade
immediately tout de suite
import importer
important important(e)
impossible impossible
impressive impressionnant(e)
improve améliorer
included compris(e)
income revenu (m.)
increase (vb.) augmenter
increase augmentation (f.)
inexpensive pas cher
information renseignement(s) (m.)
injured blessé(e)
interesting intéressant(e)

interpreter interprète (m. and f.)
invite inviter
invoice facture (f.)
Ireland Irlande (f.)
Irish irlandais(e)

jacket veste (f.)
jam confiture (f.)
Japan Japon (m.)
Japanese japonais(e)
job emploi (m.), poste (m.)
journalist journaliste (m. and f.)

keep (vb.) garder
key clé (f.)
kind aimable
kitchen cuisine (f.)
knife couteau (m.)
knock (vb.) frapper
know savoir (irreg.), connaître (irreg.)

lady dame
lake lac (m.)
lamp lampe (f.)
land terre (f.)
language langue (f.)
large grand(e)
last dernier, dernière
late en retard
law loi (f.)
lawyer avocat (m.), -e (f.)
learn apprendre (irreg.)
leather cuir (m.)
leave (vb.) partir (irreg.),
  quitter
lecture conférence (f.)
left: on/to the left à gauche
leg jambe (f.)
less moins
lesson leçon (f.)
letter lettre (f.)
library bibliothèque (f.)
life vie (f.)
lift ascenseur (m.)
like (vb.) aimer
listen (to) écouter

live habiter, vivre (irreg.)
long long, longue
look (at) regarder
look for chercher
lose perdre
loud fort(e)
luck chance (f.)
luggage bagages (m. usu.pl.)
lunch déjeuner (m.)

machine appareil (m.), machine (f.)
magazine revue (f.)
mail courrier (m.)
main principal(e)
make faire (irreg.)
managing director (and chairman) président-directeur général (m.), présidente-directrice générale (f.)
many beaucoup (de)
map carte (f.), plan (m.)
market marché (m.)
marriage mariage (m.)
married marié(e)
  to get married se marier
match (sport) match (m.)
match (light) allumette (f.)
me me, moi
meal repas (m.)
meat viande (f.)
mechanic mécanicien (m.), -ienne (f.)
medicine médicament (m.)
meet rencontrer
meeting réunion (f.)
message message (m.)
method méthode (f.)
midday midi (m.)
midnight minuit (m.)
milk lait (m.)
mine mien (m.), mienne (f.)
mistake erreur (f.)
  to make a mistake se tromper
mobile phone portable (m.)
modern moderne
moment instant, moment (m.)

money argent (m.)
month mois (m.)
mood humeur (f.)
more plus
morning matin (m.)
mother mère
motorcycle moto (f.)
motorist automobiliste (m. and f.)
mountain montagne (f.)
much beaucoup (de)
  as much/many autant (de)
  so much/many tant (de)
museum musée (m.)
music musique (f.)
must (to have to) devoir (irreg.)
my mon, ma, mes

name nom (m.)
napkin serviette (f.)
near près (adv.) près de (prep.)
necessary nécessaire
neighbor voisin (m.), -e (f.)
nephew neveu
never jamais, ne [verb] jamais
new neuf, neuve (f.), nouveau, nouvelle
news nouvelle(s) (f.)
newspaper journal (m.)
next prochain(e)
next to à côté de
niece nièce
night nuit (f.)
night club boîte (f.) de nuit
no non
no longer ne [verb] plus
no one personne, ne [verb] personne
noise bruit (m.)
noisy bruyant(e)
normal normal(e)
north nord (m.)
nose nez (m.)
note (message) petit mot (m.)
nothing rien, ne [verb] rien
now maintenant
number numéro (m.)
nurse infirmier (m.), -ière (f.)

obey obéir
obtain obtenir (irreg.)
obvious évident(e)
occasionally de temps en temps
occupied occupé(e)
odd bizarre
of de
offend offenser
offer offre (f.)
office bureau
often souvent
oil huile (f.)
old vieux, vieille
on sur
only seul(e), seulement
open (vb.) ouvrir (irreg.) j'ouvre,
  nous ouvrons; j'ai ouvert
open ouvert(e)
opinion avis (m.)
  in my opinion à mon avis
opportunity occasion (f.)
or ou
order (vb.) commander
  in order to pour, afin de
ordinary ordinaire
organize organiser
other autre
our notre, nos
ours le/la nôtre, les nôtres
overlook donner sur
overtime heures (f.) supplémentaires

pack (vb.) (luggage) faire ses
  valises (f. pl.)
pain douleur (f.)
paint (vb.) peindre (irreg.)
paper papier (m.)
park parc (m.)
party fête (f.)
passport passeport (m.)
patient patient (m.), -e (f.)
pay (for) payer
pen stylo (m.)
  pen (ballpoint) stylo (m.) bille
pencil crayon (m.)
people gens (m. pl.)

perfect (vb.) perfectionner
perfume parfum (m.)
perhaps peut-être
permit (vb.) permettre (irreg.)
persuade persuader
photograph photo (f.)
photograph (vb.) prendre
  en photo
pharmacy pharmacie (f.)
pick up (signals) capter
plan projet (m.)
plane avion (m.)
play (vb.) jouer
pleasant agréable
please s'il te/vous plaît
please (vb.) plaire (irreg.)
pleased content(e)
pleasure plaisir (m.)
pocket poche (f.)
police officer policier (m.),
  -ière (f.)
polite poli(e)
poor pauvre
possible possible
post office bureau (m.) de poste
postcard carte (f.) postale
postman/-woman facteur (m.),
  -trice (f.)
postpone reporter
practice pratiquer
prefer préférer
prepare préparer
prescription ordonnance (f.)
press presse (f.)
press conference conférence (f.)
  de presse
pretty joli(e)
prevent empêcher
price prix (m.)
probable probable
product produit (m.)
profession profession (f.)
prohibit interdire, défendre
promise (vb.) promettre (irreg.)
psychology psychologie (f.)
purse (coin) porte-monnaie (m.)

put mettre (irreg.)
qualifications diplômes (m. pl.)
quality qualité (f.)
quarrel dispute (f.)
quarrel (vb.) se disputer
queen reine
question question (f.)
  to ask a question poser une
  question
quick rapide
quickly vite, rapidement
quiet calme

rabies rage (f.)
radio radio (f.)
railway station gare (f.)
rain (vb.) pleuvoir (irreg.)
  it is raining il pleut
  it rained il a plu
rapid rapide
rash (skin) éruption (f.)
razor rasoir (m.)
read lire (irreg.)
ready prêt(e)
realize se rendre compte de
reason raison (f.)
reasonable raisonnable
receive recevoir (irreg.) je reçois,
  il reçoit, n. recevons, ils reçoivent;
  j'ai reçu, je recevrai
recently récemment
recommend recommander
record (vinyl) disque (m.)
refuse (vb.) refuser
regret (vb.) regretter
remember se souvenir de (irreg.,
  conj. like venir)
repair (vb.) réparer
repeat répéter
reply (vb.) répondre
rescue services les secours (m.)
reserve réserver
rest (vb.) se reposer
restaurant restaurant (m.)
return (vb.) retourner, rentrer
rich riche

right correct(e)
  on/to the right à droite
  to be right avoir raison
room salle (f.)
  bedroom chambre (f.)
Russia Russie (f.)
Russian russe

sad triste
safe (valuables) coffre-fort (m.)
sailing: to go sailing faire de la voile
salad salade (f.)
salary salaire (m.)
sale vente (f.)
sales (bargains) soldes (m. pl.)
sales assistant vendeur (m.),
  -euse (f.)
sand sable (m.)
say dire (irreg.)
Scotland Écosse (f.)
Scottish écossais(e)
sea mer (f.)
seat place (f.)
secretary secrétaire (m. and f.)
see voir (irreg.)
sell vendre
send envoyer (irreg.)
serious grave
serve servir (irreg.)
settle régler
several plusieurs
shame (pity) dommage (m.)
  What a shame! Quel dommage!
shave (vb.) raser, se raser
shirt chemise (f.)
shop magasin (m.), boutique (f.)
shop window vitrine (f.)
shopkeeper commerçant (m.), -e (f.)
shopping courses (f. pl.)
short court(e)
show spectacle (m.)
show (vb.) montrer
shut (vb.) fermer
sign (vb.) signer
since depuis; puisque
sing chanter

single (ticket) aller (m.) simple;
  (room) chambre (f.) individuelle;
  (unmarried) célibataire
sister sœur
sit down s'asseoir (irreg.)
size taille (f.)
skate (vb.) faire du patin/roller
skating rink patinoire (f.)
ski (vb.) faire du ski
skirt jupe (f.)
sleep (vb.) dormir (irreg.) je dors,
  il dort, nous dormons; j'ai dormi
sleeping bag sac (m.) de couchage
slowly lentement
small petit(e)
smell (vb.) sentir (irreg.)
smoke (vb.) fumer
snow (vb.) neiger
so si, aussi; donc
some du (m.), de la (f.)
something quelque chose
son fils
soon bientôt
  as soon as aussitôt que
sorry désolé(e)
soup soupe (f.)
south sud (m.)
Spain Espagne (f.)
Spanish espagnol(e)
speak parler
speaker (smart) enceinte (f.)
  (connectée)
special offer promotion (f.)
spend (money) dépenser
spend (time) passer
spoon cuillère (f.)
sport sport (m.)
square place (f.)
stamp timbre (m.)
stand in line (vb.) faire la queue
start (vb.) commencer
station gare, station (f.)
stay (vb.) rester
still encore, toujours
stop s'arrêter, cesser
straight ahead tout droit
street rue (f.)

street map plan (m.)
student
  (university) étudiant (m.) ,-e (f.);
  (other) élève (m. and f.)
study (vb.) étudier
stylish chic
succeed réussir
sugar sucre (m.)
suit costume (m.)
suitcase valise (f.)
sun soleil (m.)
sunglasses lunettes (f.) de soleil
supermarket supermarché (m.)
surprise (vb.) surprendre (irreg.)
sure sûr(e)
survey enquête (f.)
swim nager, se baigner
swimming pool piscine (f.)

tablet comprimé (m.)
take prendre (irreg.)
  take down descendre
  take part participer
  take place avoir lieu
  take up monter
tall grand(e)
tea thé (m.)
telephone (vb.) téléphoner
tell dire (irreg.)
tent tente (f.)
terrible affreux, -euse
thank remercier
that/this ce (m.), cette (f.)
theft vol (m.)
their leur, leurs
there là, y
these/those ces (m. and f.)
think penser
thirsty, to be thirsty avoir soif
ticket billet (m.)
tidy (vb.) ranger
time temps (m.); heure (f.); fois (f.)
timetable horaire (m.)
tip (gratuity) pourboire (m.)
tire pneu (m.)
tired fatigué(e)
today aujourd'hui

toilet toilettes (f. pl.)
tomorrow demain
too trop
too much/many trop (de)
tooth dent (f.)
towel serviette (f.)
town ville (f.)
train train (m.)
translation traduction (f.)
travel (vb.) voyager
truck camion (m.)
try (vb.) essayer

ugly laid(e)
umbrella parapluie (m.)
unable: I am unable to pay je ne
  peux pas payer
under sous
understand comprendre (irreg.)
unemployed au chômage
unfair injuste
unfortunately malheureusement
unhappy malheureux, -euse
United States États-Unis (m. pl.)
until jusqu'à, jusqu'à ce que
upstairs en haut
USB flashdrive clé (f.) USB
usually d'habitude
use (vb.) utiliser

vacancies (hotel) chambres libres
vacate (room) libérer
vacation vacances (f. pl.)
valid valable
valuables objets (m. pl.) de valeur
vegetable légume (m.)
view vue (f.)
  view over the sea vue sur mer
visit (vb.) visiter

wait (for) attendre
waiter serveur (m.), -euse (f.)
wake up réveiller, se réveiller
Wales pays (m.) de Galles
walk (vb.) marcher
  to go for a walk se promener

wallet porte-feuille (m.)
want (vb.) vouloir (irreg.)
warm, to be warm avoir chaud
wash (vb.) laver, se laver
watch (vb.) regarder
watch over surveiller
watch (wrist) montre (f.)
water eau (f.)
  drinking water eau potable
waterskiing ski (m.) nautique
wave vague (f.)
wear (vb.) porter
week semaine (f.)
well bien
Welsh gallois(e)
west ouest (m.)
what quel (m.), quelle (f.)
wheel roue (f.)
when quand
where où
which quel (m.), quelle (f.),
  que (rel pron.)
white blanc, blanche
who, whom qui
why pourquoi
wife femme, épouse
wind vent (m.)
windsurfing planche (f.) à voile
wine vin (m.)
wish (vb.) désirer, souhaiter
wonderful magnifique
word mot (m.)
work (vb.) travailler; **(of
  machines)** marcher
write écrire (irreg.)
wrong: to be wrong avoir tort

year an (m.)
yesterday hier
young jeune
your ton (m. fam.), ta (f. fam.),
  votre
yours tien(ne), le/la tien(ne), le
  vôtre

accord (m.) agreement
  je suis d'accord I agree
acheter to buy
acteur/-trice actor
addition (f.) bill
adresse (f.) address
affaire (f.) matter
  c'est une bonne affaire it's a bargain (good buy)
affaires (f. pl.) business
  homme/femme d'affaires businessperson
affreux/-euse dreadful
afin de in order to
agence (f.) agency
agréable pleasant
aider to help
aimable kind
aimer to like, love
alcool (m.) alcohol
Allemagne (f.) Germany
allemand(e) German
aller (irreg.) to go
allumette (f.) match (light)
ambassade (f.) embassy
ambulance (f.) ambulance
ambulancier/-ière ambulance driver
améliorer to improve
amener to bring (sec. 12.5)
américain(e) American
Amérique (f.) America
ami(e) friend
amuser to amuse
  s'amuser to enjoy oneself
an (m.) year
analyser to analyze
anglais(e) English
Angleterre (f.) England
annonce (f.) advertisement
annoncer to announce
annuler to cancel
antiquaire (m. and f.) antique dealer
appareil (m.) machine

appareil-photo (m.) camera
appartement (m.) apartment
appeler to call
  s'appeler to be called
apporter to bring
apprécier to appreciate
apprendre (irreg.) to learn
approuver to approve (of)
après after
après-midi (m. or f.) afternoon
argent (m.) money
arrêter, s'arrêter to stop
arriver to arrive; to happen
ascenseur (m.) elevator (lift)
asseoir, s'asseoir (irreg.) to sit down
assez enough; fairly
astronaute (m. and f.) astronaut
attacher to attach
attendre to wait (for)
au-dessus de above
augmenter to increase
augmentation (f.) increase
aujourd'hui today
au revoir goodbye
aussi also
aussitôt que as soon as
autant (de) as much/many
autobus (m.) bus
automobiliste (m. and f.) motorist
autoroute (f.) highway
autre other
avance: à l'avance in advance
avant before
avion (m.) airplane
avis (m.) opinion
  à mon avis in my opinion
avocat(e) lawyer
avoir (irreg.) to have
  avoir lieu to take place

bagages (m. pl.) luggage
baigner, se baigner to have a swim
bain (m.) bath

banque (f.) bank
banquier/-ière banker
bar (m.) bar
bas, basse (f.) low
   en bas downstairs
bateau (m.) boat
beau/belle beautiful
beaucoup (de) much/many
Belgique (f.) Belgium
bibliothèque (f.) library
bien well
bien que (+subj.) although
bientôt soon
bière (f.) beer
bilingue bilingual
billet (m.) ticket
bizarre odd
blanc, blanche white
blessé(e) injured
bleu(e) blue
boire (irreg.) to drink
boîte (f.) box
   boîte de nuit nightclub
bon, bonne good
boucherie (f.) butcher shop
boulangerie (f.) bakery
bouteille (f.) bottle
bras (m.) arm
britannique British
brochure (f.) brochure
brouillard (m.) fog
bruit (m.) noise
brûler to burn
brun(e) brown
bruyant(e) noisy

cadeau (m.) gift
café (m.) coffee; café
caisse (f.) cash register, till
calme calm, quiet
cambrioleur/-euse burglar
camion (m.) truck
camper to camp
Canada (m.) Canada

capter to pick up/capture (signals)
car (m.) coach
carte (f.) card; map
carte de crédit credit card
carte postale postcard
casser to break
cathédrale (f.) cathedral
ce, cette, etc. this
celui, celle, etc. the one
célèbre famous
cesser to stop
chaise (f.) chair
chaise longue deckchair
chambre (f.) bedroom
champ (m.) field
chance (f.) luck
changer to change
chanter to sing
chapeau (m.) hat
chaque each
château (m.) castle
chaud(e) hot
   avoir chaud to be hot, warm
   il fait chaud it's warm (weather)
chemise (f.) shirt
chemise de nuit nightshirt
chèque (m.) check
cher, chère expensive
chercher to look for
cheveux (m. pl.) hair (on head)
chic stylish, classy
Chine (f.) China
choisir to choose
chômage (m.) unemployment
   au chômage unemployed
clé (f.) key
   clé (f.) USB USB flashdrive
client(e) customer
climatisation (f.) air-conditioning
cœur (m.) heart
coffre-fort (m.) safe (box)
coiffeur/-euse hairdresser
combien how much/many
commander to order

commencer to begin
comment how
commerçant(e) shopkeeper
compagnie (f.) aérienne airline company
composer (un numéro) to dial
comprendre (irreg.) to understand
comprimé (m.) tablet
compris(e) included
conducteur/-trice driver
conduire (irreg.) to drive
conférence (f.) conference; lecture
confirmer to confirm
confiture (f.) jam
confortable comfortable
connaître (irreg.) to know
conseiller to advise
construire (irreg.) to build
consulter to consult
content(e) pleased
continuer to continue
contrat (m.) contract
copier to copy
correct(e) correct
corriger to correct
costume (m.) suit
côté (m.) side
  à côté de next to
couleur (f.) color
couper to cut
courageux/-euse brave
courrier (m.) mail
courses (f. pl.) shopping
court(e) short
couteau (m.) knife
coûter to cost
crayon (m.) pencil
créer to create
critiquer to criticize
cuillère (f.) spoon
cuir (m.) leather
cuisine (f.) kitchen; cooking

dame lady
dangereux/-euse dangerous
danser to dance
date (f.) date
débarquer to disembark
décider to decide
décourager to discourage
défendre to defend; to forbid
déjà already
déjeuner (m.) lunch
  petit déjeuner breakfast
délicieux/-euse delicious
demain tomorrow
demander to ask (for)
dent (f.) tooth
dentiste (m. and f.) dentist
départ (m.) departure
dépêcher (se) to hurry
dépenser to spend (money)
depuis since
déranger to disturb
dernier, dernière last
derrière behind
descendre to go down; to take down
désirer to wish
désolé(e) sorry
détester to hate
devant in front of
devoir (irreg.) to have to (must)
dictionnaire (m.) dictionary
difficile difficult
dîner (m.) dinner
diplôme (m.) diploma
dire (irreg.) to say, tell
directeur/-trice director
discuter de to discuss
dispute (f.) quarrel
  se disputer to quarrel
disque (m.) record
divertissement (m.) entertainment
docteur(e) doctor
dommage shame, pity
  quel dommage what a shame

donc so, therefore

donner to give

donner sur to overlook (view)

dormir (irreg.) to sleep
  je dors, il dort, n. dormons,
  j'ai dormi

douane (f.) customs

douanier/-ière customs officer

douleur (f.) pain

douter to doubt

drapeau (m.) flag

droit: tout droit straight ahead

droite: à droite on/to the right

du, de la, etc. some (sec. 1.1)

eau (f.) water
  eau potable drinking water

écossais(e) Scottish

Écosse (f.) Scotland

écouter to listen (to)

écrire (irreg.) to write

écriture (f.) handwriting

efficace efficient

église (f.) church

électricien(ne) electrician

élève (m. and f.) student, pupil

émission (f.) broadcast

empêcher to prevent

emploi (m.) job

enceinte (f.) (connectée)
  (smart) speaker

encore again; still; yet

encourager to encourage

énergie (f.) energy

énervant(e) annoying

ennuyeux/-euse boring; annoying
  s'ennuyer to be bored

enquête (f.) survey, investigation

ensuite afterward

entendre to hear

entre between

entrer to enter

enveloppe (f.) envelope

envoyer (irreg.) to send

épicerie (f.) food shop, deli

époux, épouse spouse

erreur (f.) mistake

éruption (f.) rash (skin)

Espagne (f.) Spain

espagnol(e) Spanish

espérer to hope

essayer to try

essence (f.) gasoline

est (m.) east

et and

États-Unis (m. pl.) United States

étranger, étrangère foreign
  à l'étranger abroad

être (irreg.) to be

étudiant(e) student (university)

étudier to study

évident(e) obvious

éviter to avoid

exactement exactly

excellent(e) excellent

excursion (f.) excursion

explication (f.) explanation

exporter to export

face: en face de across from

facile easy

facteur/-trice postman/
  postwoman

facture (f.) invoice

faim (f.) hunger
  avoir faim to be hungry

faire (irreg.) to do, make

falloir (irreg.) to be necessary; need
  il nous faut partir we must leave;
  il nous faut 50 euros we need 50
  euros

famille (f.) family

fatigué(e) tired

faut see **falloir**

fauteuil (m.) armchair

féliciter to congratulate

femme woman; wife

fermer to shut

fête (f.) party, festival
fièvre (f.) fever
fille daughter, girl
  jeune fille young girl
film (m.) film
fils son
fin (f.) end
finir to finish
fois (f.) time (occasion)
fort(e) strong; loud
fourchette (f.) fork
frais, fraîche fresh, cool
français(e) French
France (f.) France
frapper to knock
frère brother
froid(e) cold
  avoir froid to be cold
  il fait froid it's cold (weather)
fromage (m.) cheese
fruit(s) (m.) fruit
fumer to smoke

gagner to win; earn
gallois(e) Welsh
gant (m.) glove
garage (m.) garage
garantir to guarantee
garçon boy
garder to keep
gare (f.) railway station
gâteau (m.) cake
gauche: à gauche on/to the left
généralement generally
gens (m. pl.) people
glace (f.) ice; ice cream
gouvernement (m.) government
grand(e) big, tall
Grande-Bretagne (f.) Britain
gratuit(e) free (of charge)
grave serious
Grèce (f.) Greece
gris(e) gray
groupe (m.) group

guide (m.) guide;
  guidebook

habiter to live
habitude (f.) habit
  d'habitude usually
haut(e) high
  en haut upstairs
heure (f.) hour
  heures supplémentaires
  overtime
heureux/-euse happy
heureusement fortunately
hier yesterday
homme man
hôpital (m.) hospital
horaire (m.) timetable
hôtel (m.) hotel
huile (f.) oil
humeur (f.) mood

ici here
il y a there is/are; ago
important(e) important
importer to import
impossible impossible
impressionnant(e) impressive
incendie (m.) fire
infirmier/-ière nurse
ingénieur(e) engineer
injuste unfair
instant (m.) moment
interdire to forbid, to prohibit
intéressant(e) interesting
interprète (m. and f.) interpreter
inviter to invite
irlandais(e) Irish
Irlande (f.) Ireland

jamais, ne [verb] jamais never
jambe (f.) leg
jambon (m.) ham
Japon (m.) Japan
japonais(e) Japanese

jardin (m.) garden
jeune young
joli(e) pretty
jouer to play
journal (m.) newspaper
journaliste (m. and f.) journalist
jupe (f.) skirt
jusqu'à as far as; until

là there
lac (m.) lake
laid(e) ugly
lait (m.) milk
lampe (f.) lamp
langue (f.) tongue; language
laver to wash
  se laver to wash oneself
leçon (f.) lesson
légume vegetable
lentement slowly
lettre (f.) letter
leur their
  le leur theirs
lever to raise
  se lever to get up
libérer to free, vacate
librairie (f.) bookstore
libre free (available)
lire (irreg.) to read
lit (m.) bed
livre (m.) book
livre (f.) pound sterling
logiciel (m.) software
loi (f.) law
loin far, long
long, longue long
louer to hire
lourd heavy
lunettes (f. pl.) spectacles
  lunettes de soleil sunglasses

machine (f.) machine
magasin (m.) shop
magnifique wonderful

main (f.) hand
maintenant now
mais but
maison (f.) house
mal badly
malade ill
maladie (f.) illness
malheureux/-euse unhappy
malheureusement unfortunately
La Manche (f.) Channel
manger to eat
marchander to haggle
marché (m.) market
marcher to walk
mari husband
mariage (m.) marriage
marié(e) married
marier: se marier to get married
marque (f.) brand
match (m.) match (sport)
matin (m.) morning
mauvais(e) bad
mécanicien(ne) mechanic
médecin (m. and f.) doctor
médicament (m.) medicine
meilleur(e) better
même same; even
mer (f.) sea
mère mother
message (m.) message
méthode (f.) method
mettre (irreg.) to put
midi (m.) midday
mien(ne), le/la mien(ne) mine
mieux better
minuit (m.) midnight
mode (f.) fashion
moderne modern
moi me
  avec/pour moi with/for me
moins less
mois (m.) month
moitié (f.) half
mon, ma, mes my

montagne (f.) mountain
monter to go up; take up
montre (f.) watch
montrer to show
mouchoir (m.) tissue (facial),
  handkerchief
mot (m.) word
  un petit mot a note
moteur (m.) engine
moto (f.) motorcycle
musée (m.) museum
musique (f.) music

nager to swim
nécessaire necessary
neiger to snow
nettoyer to clean
neuf, neuve brand new
neveu nephew
nez (m.) nose
nièce niece
noir(e) black
nom (m.) name
non no
nord (m.) north
normal(e) normal
note (f.) bill
notre, nos our
  le nôtre ours
nourriture (f.) food
nouveau, nouvelle new
nouvelle(s) (f.) news
nuit (f.) night
  boîte (f.) de nuit nightclub
numéro (m.) number

obéir to obey
obtenir (irreg.) to obtain
occasion (f.) opportunity
  une voiture d'occ. a used car
occupé(e) busy
offenser to offend
offre (f.) offer
opéra (m.) opera

ordinaire ordinary
ordinateur (m.) computer
ordonnance (f.) prescription
organiser to organize
ou or
où where
oublier to forget
ouest (m.) west
ouvrir (irreg.) to open
  j'ouvre, il ouvre, n. ouvrons,
  j'ai ouvert
ouvert(e) open

pain (m.) bread
pain grillé toast
panne (f.) breakdown
papier (m.) paper
parapluie (m.) umbrella
parc (m.) park
parce que because
pardonner to forgive
parfum (m.) perfume
parler to speak
participer to take part
partir (irreg.) to leave
partout everywhere
passeport (m.) passport
passer to spend (time)
patient(e) patient
patinoire (f.) skating rink
  faire du patin to ice skate
patron(ne) owner, boss
pauvre poor
payer to pay (for)
  payer en espèces to pay in cash
pays (m.) country
pays (m.) de Galles Wales
pêche (f.) peach
pêche (f.) fishing
  aller à la pêche to go fishing
peindre (irreg.) to paint
penser to think
perdre to lose
père father

perfectionner to perfect
permettre (irreg.) to allow
permis (m.) license
  per. de conduire driver's license
personne (f.) person
  ne [verb] personne no one
persuader to persuade
petit(e) small
peut-être perhaps
pharmacie (f.) pharmacy (chemist)
photo (f.) photograph
  prendre en p. to take a photo
pièce (f.) d'identité identification
piscine (f.) swimming pool
place (f.) place, seat; square
plage (f.) beach
plainte (f.) complaint
plaire (irreg.) to please, to be
  pleasing
s'il te/vous plaît please
plaisir (m.) pleasure
plan (m.) street map
planche (f.) à voile windsurfing
  board
  faire de la planche à voile
  to windsurf
plat (m.) dish
plein(e) full
pleuvoir (irreg.) to rain
  il pleut it's raining
  il a plu it rained
plonger to dive
plus more
  ne [verb] plus no more/no longer
plusieurs several
pneu (m.) tire
poche (f.) pocket
poisson (m.) fish
poissonnerie (f.) fishmonger's
poli(e) polite
police (f.) police
  policier/-ière police officer
pomme (f.) apple
pomme de terre potato

pompiers (m. pl.) firefighters
port (m.) port, harbor
portable (m.) mobile phone
  ordinateur portable (m.) laptop
porte-feuille (m.) wallet
porte-monnaie (m.) coin purse
porter to carry; wear
possible possible
poste (m.) job
poste (f.) post office
pour for; in order to
pourboire (m.) tip (gratuity)
pourquoi why
pouvoir (irreg.) to be able (can)
pratiquer to practice
préférer to prefer
premier, première first
prendre (irreg.) to take
préparer to prepare
près de near
président(e)-directeur/-trice
  général(e)
  chairman and managing director
presse (f.) press
  conférence de presse
  press conference
prêt(e) ready
principal(e) main
prix (m.) price
probable probable
prochain(e) next
produit (m.) product
profession (f.) profession
profond(e) deep
projet (m.) plan
promener to take for a walk (12.5)
  se promener to go for a walk
promettre (irreg.) to promise
promotion (f.) special offer
psychologie (f.) psychology
publicité (f.) advertising
puisque since, because

qualité (f.) quality
quand when
que (interrog.) what
que (rel. pron.) whom/which
quel(le) which/what
quelque chose something
question (f.) question
  poser une question to ask a
  question
qui (interrog.) who
qui (rel. pron.) who/which
quitter to leave
quoique (+ subj) although

radio (f.) radio
rage (f.) rabies
raison (f.) reason
  avoir raison to be right
raisonnable reasonable
ranger to tidy
rapidement quickly
raser to shave
  se raser to shave oneself
rasoir (m.) razor
récemment recently
recevoir (irreg.) to receive
  **je reçois, il reçoit, nous
  recevons, ils reçoivent, j'ai
  reçu, je recevrai**
recommander to recommend
refuser to refuse
regarder to look (at), watch
régime (m.) diet
régler to settle
regretter to regret
reine queen
remercier to thank
remplir to fill
rencontrer to meet
rendez-vous (m.) appointment
rendre to give back
renouvelable renewable
renseignment(s) information
rentrer to return

réparer to repair
repas (m.) meal
répéter to repeat
répondre to reply
reporter (m. and f.) reporter (news)
reporter to take back;
  postpone
reposer, se reposer to rest
réserver to book
restaurant (m.) restaurant
rester to stay
retard (m.) lateness
  en retard late
retourner to return
réunion (f.) meeting
réussir to succeed
réveiller, se réveiller to wake up
revenu (m.) income
revue (f.) magazine
rhume (m.) cold
  rhume des foins hayfever
riche rich
rien: ne [verb] rien nothing
robe (f.) dress
roue (f.) wheel
rouler to drive
rue (f.) street
russe Russian
Russie (f.) Russia

sable (m.) sand
sac (m.) bag
  sac à main handbag
  sac de couchage sleeping bag
salade (f.) salad
salaire (m.) salary
sale dirty
salle (f.) room
santé (f.) health
savoir (irreg.) to know
secours (m.) rescue services
secrétaire (m. and f.) secretary
semaine (f.) week
serveur/-euse waiter/waitress

serviette (f.) napkin; towel
servir (irreg.) to serve
seul(e) alone; only
seulement only
sien, le sien his/hers/its
signer to sign
ski (m.) skiing
  ski nautique water-skiing
  faire du ski to go skiing
sœur sister
soif (f.) thirst
  avoir soif to be thirsty
soir (m.) evening
soldes (m. pl.) sales (bargains)
soleil (m.) sun
  lunettes (f. pl.) de soleil
  sunglasses
son, sa, ses his/her/its
sortie (f.) exit
  sortie de secours fire exit
sortir (irreg.) to go out;
  take out
souhaiter to wish, to want
soupe (f.) soup
sous under
souvenir (m.) souvenir; memory
se souvenir de (conj. like venir)
  to remember
souvent often
spectacle (m.) show
sport (m.) sport
stand in line (f.) queue
  faire la queue to stand in line
stylo (m.) pen
  stylo bille ballpoint pen
sucre (m.) sugar
sud (m.) south
supermarché (m.) supermarket
supplément (m.) extra
sur on
sûr(e) sure
surprendre (irreg.) to surprise
surtout especially
surveiller to watch over

taille (f.) size; waist
tant (de) so much/many
tante aunt
tasse (f.) cup
téléphone (m.) telephone
téléphoner to telephone
temps (m.) time
  de temps en temps occasionally
tension (f.) stress; blood pressure
tente (f.) tent
terre (f.) land
tête (f.) head
thé (m.) tea
tien(ne), le/la tien(ne) yours
(fam.)
timbre (m.) stamp
toilettes (f. pl.) toilet
tomber to fall
  tomber en panne to break down
ton, ta, tes your (fam.)
tort: avoir tort to be wrong
tôt early
toujours always; still
tout all, everything
tout le monde everyone
tout de suite immediately
traduction (f.) translation
train (m.) train
travailler to work
traverser to cross
triste sad
tromper to deceive
  se tromper to make a mistake
trop too
trop (de) too much/many
trouver to find

Union (f.) européenne
  European Union
urgence (f.) emergency
  en cas d'urgence in an
  emergency
utiliser to use

vacances (f. pl.) vacations
vague (f.) wave
valable valid
valeur (f.) value
   objets de valeur valuables
valise (f.) suitcase
   faires ses valises to pack
vélo (m.) bike
vendeur/-euse sales assistant
vendre to sell
venir (irreg.) to come
vent (m.) wind
vente (f.) sale
vérifier to check
verre (m.) glass
verser to pour; pay
   verser un acompte (m.) to leave
   a deposit
veste (f.) jacket
vêtements (m. pl.) clothes

viande (f.) meat
vie (f.) life
vieux, vieille old
ville (f.) town
vin (m.) wine
visiter to visit
vitrine (f.) shop window
vivre (irreg.) to live
voici here is/are
voile (f.) sail
   faire de la voile to go sailing
voir (irreg.) to see
voisin(e) neighbor
voiture (f.) car
vol (m.) flight; theft
votre your; le/la vôtre yours
vouloir (irreg.) to want
voyager to travel
vue (f.) view

Index

The numbers refer to section headings, unless pages are specified.